Urban Network:
Museums Embracing Communities

Edited *by*

Jennifer Amdur Spitz and Margaret Thom
of Amdur Spitz & Associates

Published *by*

The Field Museum, Chicago, Illinois

Made possible by the National Recreation Foundation

Urban Network: Museums Embracing Communities is made possible by the National Recreation Foundation through *The Diversity Project: Increasing Equity of Access: Igniting a National Discussion*, a two-year grant to The Field Museum. The National Recreation Foundation is dedicated to developing opportunities for those who do not have access to recreation programs.

Acknowledgments

Bronwyn Bevan, Mike Bradecich, Robert W. Crawford, Jr., Beth Crownover, Norma Dolcater, Robert Eskridge, Sumita Goel, Charles Hartsoe, Barbara Henry, Joel Hoffman, Karen Ransom Lehman, Patricia Williams Lessane, Alisa Martin, John W. McCarter, Jr., Lisa Meyerowitz, Tony Mobley, Paul Mohrbacher, Mariet Morgan, Mary Ellen Munley, Nicole Neal, Karen Nelson, Lisa Rebori, Paul Richard, Carolee Smith Rogers, Beth B. Schneider, Sarah Schultz, Susan Schwartzenberg, Kiyoko Motoyama Sims, Sophia Siskel, Jean Sousa, Jennifer Amdur Spitz, Mary Ann Steiner, Carolyn Sumners, Encarnación Teurel, Margaret Thom, Ellen Wahl

Contents

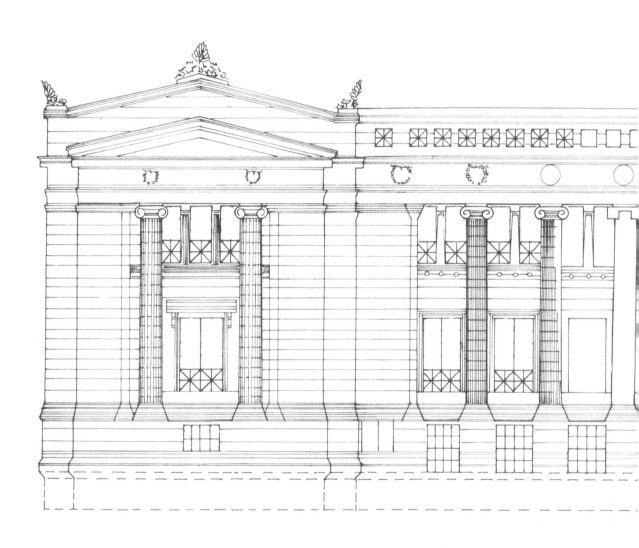

Section 1 Introduction

Introduction

Jennifer Amdur Spitz and Margaret Thom

Urban Network: Museums Embracing Communities seeks to improve the equality of access to museum learning for all people. The consortium consists of ten major museums in five metropolitan areas across the United States that have innovative programs and strategies to attract, serve, and engage diverse audiences. Urban Network members share effective practices, strategies, and resources and advance a national dialogue on civic engagement.

Background

In recent years, museums have been increasingly interested in attracting and building deeper relationships with more diverse audiences. A plethora of innovative programs has evolved. These programs and the relationships museums have forged with communities have created new ways for audiences to participate in museum learning and to some degree have impacted the nature of museum collections and exhibitions. Recent census figures highlight the changing face of the American public and reinforce the importance of museums and other cultural institutions to serve increasingly diverse demographics.

The American Association of Museums (AAM) elevated its diversity coalition to an administrative committee of the board. The AAM also launched the Museums and Community Initiative to explore the potential for dynamic engagement between American communities and their museums and published *Mastering Civic Engagement: A Challenge to Museums.* Several foundations, most notably the Wallace-Reader's Digest Funds and The Pew Charitable Trusts, have supported community engagement programs by art museums during the past decade to develop and diversify audiences. In the world of science, donors, such as the National Science Foundation, Annenberg Foundation and the Howard Hughes Medical Institute, have supported formal and informal education initiatives, as well as career development programs. Many of these initiatives have focused on partnerships with schools and online learning.

NRF Grant

In 2000, The Field Museum secured funding from the National Recreation Foundation (NRF) to expand its partnerships with community-based organizations in conjunction with its summer camp program. NRF also sponsored The Field to convene a national consortium that would begin a dialogue about how to increase access for diverse audiences and disseminate the proceedings from their meetings.

The Field Museum engaged Amdur Spitz & Associates, a national communications consulting firm with strong expertise in helping large institutions connect to community, to lead the formation of the national consortium and the publication of this book.

Consortium Goals

- To improve equality of access to museum learning for all people
- To offer welcoming museum experiences that encourage first-time visitors to return again and again
- To increase participation by individuals and communities traditionally underserved by museums

Objectives

- To begin a national conversation with colleagues from urban museums that focuses on the many complex issues related to equality of access
- To speed learning by sharing and collaborating so that consortium member museums can improve existing programs and initiatives and share successful practices with others

Purpose

- To build a sustainable, nationwide network of museums that use innovative methods to increase audience diversity and participation in museum learning
- To bring attention to issues of access
- To facilitate sharing of information, strategies, and effective practices
- To create a place where museums can discuss barriers and create solutions for accessibility issues
- To share successful strategies and models which have worked to build new audiences and deepen relationships with former non-users, as well as to facilitate adapting those models to other consortium museum environments
- To assist consortium members in gaining support and resources to implement ideas and adapt models learned through the consortium network
- To recognize individuals and institutions providing significant contributions to this field

Consortium Members

The members of Urban Network, arranged by city, are as follows:

Chicago	• The Art Institute of Chicago
	• The Field Museum
New York	• American Museum of Natural History
	• The Brooklyn Museum of Art
San Francisco/Bay Area	• Exploratorium
	• Oakland Museum of California
Minneapolis/St. Paul	• Science Museum of Minnesota
	• Walker Art Center
Houston	• Houston Museum of Natural Science
	• The Museum of Fine Arts, Houston

A Working Definition of Diversity

The Urban Network adopted the following definition of *diversity*:
Audience diversification programs strive to ensure equity of access to museum
learning for all people. These programs are designed to help museums better
serve audiences that reflect the demographics of an individual museum's urban
area and aim to increase participation by people traditionally underserved by the
museum. Successful programs engage these visitors to become regular museum
users. Programs seek to foster and sustain a balance of participants from diverse
racial and ethnic backgrounds and economic means. Programs may also target
people whose primary language is not English, people with different abilities,
or underrepresented age groups.

First Meeting

The first meeting of the Urban Network took place in March 2002 at The Field
Museum in Chicago. For two days two representatives from each of the ten
member museums discussed the theme: "What are the opportunities and
challenges to increasing access to museums for diverse audiences?" Participants
created the agenda and convened sessions based on their wealth of experience,
using a meeting process called Open Space Technology. Pre-meeting questions to
stimulate their discussion included:

- Reflecting upon your efforts to diversify audiences and build relationships
  with various communities, what have you learned?
- What are the elements of a successful community engagement program?
- What does a thriving, reciprocal museum-community relationship look like?
- What makes it work?
- How can we help new visitors to feel comfortable and to return?
- What do we want to do together that we cannot do alone?

The resulting 16 meeting sessions addressed a wide range of topics, including
aligning audience development with a core mission; supporting change
internally; accommodating conflicting needs among diverse audiences; engaging
new immigrant communities; using advisory groups; conducting successful artist
residencies; finding the right community partner for collaboration; evaluating
programs; and retaining and advancing people of color within museum staffs.

Through the meeting, the group established some immediate action plans and
tentative consensus on long-term actions needed to advance the field of
professionals working to improve civic engagement. In particular, the group
identified the need to craft a framework to define and further understand
diversity and community engagement. Participants sensed that museums are
being asked to change as the diversity of the United States population increases,
especially in cities. Urban Network members wanted to develop better advocacy for

community engagement within museums, better training programs for staff working with communities, and better evaluations that would help to understand the critical elements of effective practice.

Second Meeting

The second meeting, held in August 2002 at The Field Museum, provided an opportunity to deepen the work of the first meeting. Called "From Individual Experience to Shared Knowledge," the second meeting focused on two topics identified in March: documentation and evaluation of the work achieved by Urban Network members.

One working group developed an evaluation rubric for assessing the effectiveness of programs geared toward community service and diversifying audiences. Another group discussed the elemental features of program concept, design, and decision making that could be put into a "program development blueprint." The blueprint in this book is a tool synthesized from collective experience, and presented as a "how-to" manual.

This Book

This book presents the progress of the Urban Network to date. We offer these case studies as a mechanism to share with other museums and organizations examples of the community engagement programs that we have developed and what we have learned through our work both individually and together. Since the group agreed that further research is required to identify best practices, this publication seeks to document our current understanding, point the way to future initiatives, and offer practical help to others on the same path.

How to Use This Book

We hope this book catalyzes increased dialogue and debate within the museum world about how to engage communities and improve equal access to museum learning. We also hope it inspires and informs community organizations and other groups to identify ways in which they might interact, collaborate, or partner with a museum to serve their common constituents.

The essays offer reflections and experiences from individual Network members. They provide an analysis of our current situation, our work to date, and how it relates to other initiatives. They explore questions we have asked ourselves and ones that remain to be answered. They also reveal some of the complexities inherent in initiatives designed to engage diverse communities.

This book can be used as a how-to manual for building and evaluating community engagement programs. The Program Development Blueprint offers questions, considerations, and guidelines to help museums collaborate with communities and engage diverse audiences. The Evaluation Rubric guides the reader through a set of questions designed to help measure intended changes as the museum moves towards fuller civic engagement.

The case studies illustrate an innovative program at each of the member museums, including considerations on planning, developing partnerships, finding allies within the institution, overcoming obstacles, evaluating results, and identifying lessons learned. If a particular case study interests you, please contact the authoring museum for further information.

This book is also a record of the exciting and dynamic work of committed and hard-working museum professionals who gave of their time and energy to help work towards sharing their museums' ability to enrich the lives of all people.

Conclusion

Urban Network: Museums Embracing Communities has been a two-year process of building collaborative partnerships between institutions on a national level, similar to the partnership building that our members do locally. We have had our own challenges and lessons as the process of fostering trusting, reciprocal relationships is not easy for individuals, let alone institutions.

Urban Network members met in Houston in February 2003 to design the future of this consortium and our work together. The initial grant period came to a close at the end of February 2003.

Recent census data clearly illustrates how the United States population is diversifying. As the United States population changes, the success of museums' abilities to build relationships with the increasingly diverse urban communities around them will continue to impact institutional values, goals, and organizational culture. Engaging new and diverse audiences requires that museums do something different from what they have done before. Inherent in these efforts is a certain degree of risk and uncertainty in exploring new and different strategies. These are risks that museums are increasingly willing to take to remain relevant and vital centers of civic life.

Section 2 Essays

Windows onto Worlds

Bronwyn Bevan

In the nineteenth century, public museums were founded to bri~ ~-" ·
natural and man-made objects to people who otherwise would k:
lands only through books and illustrations. At a time of Western
other parts of the world, understanding and knowing these new
assimilating the new knowledge, mined like ore, was an importar
developing a shared political culture. At museums, the public vie
sarcophaguses, woolly mammoths, illuminated manuscripts, lands
West, medieval armor—objects industriously collected by a Victor
bent on exploration, appropriation, classification, and self-edificati

Education and edification were widely perceived as primary drivers of social
progress in the nineteenth century. It has been noted that public schools were
founded in the United States at about the same time as the public museum
(Hein 1998), with primers and curricula designed to develop in children a shared
view of the world, its history, and our place in it. Museums, on the other hand,
provided visitors of all ages and backgrounds with a glimpse into the "canon"
of Western historical knowledge and worldview. What is art? What is science?
What is history? The answers could all be found exhibited within museum walls.

In subsequent years, photographic images brought far-off lands and cultures
much closer to the public. Feature films, television, *National Geographic*, or *Life*
magazine took us, viscerally, to times and places previously unavailable. As our
culture became inured to the image serving as surrogate to the experience, objects
became less critical to developing an understanding of time and place. Museums
lost their perceived relevance as windows onto the world, except perhaps for those
who were predisposed to find access to and relate to the collections. Museums
became seen as elitist bastions of collections and conservation. Somewhere along
the line they all became "dusty." For decades, popular culture existed outside the
walls of most museums; inside was an object-based history book that represented a
specific cultural perspective on what constituted "the" world.

Today, and for the past few decades, museums are reinventing themselves as
public forums for the dissemination of relevant knowledge and experiences, and
sometimes as places where people can come together to create new knowledge and
culture. If the role of the museum is to provide a window onto the world, the field
grapples not only with how to best provide the window, but also with how to
effectively relate different worldviews to the collections, and vice versa.

In keeping with new research in the cognitive sciences (NRC 2000), many
museum educators consider the nature of the knowable world as one that is
constructed as much by the perceiver as by the perceived (Vygotsky 1978).
Therefore collaborations between those inside the museum and those outside the

museum have become increasingly important. Museums seek ways to have their objects or phenomena (as in the case of science museums like the Exploratorium in San Francisco) support learning and knowledge structures already in place in a variety of communities. These communities—connected by culture, age, profession, or other organizing frameworks—can make use of museum resources to deepen their own worldview and inform the museum's. The museum (in its educative role) no longer represents the canon, but the wellspring, the touchstone, the reflecting pool—caring for, investigating, and exhibiting a variety of objects or phenomena that have different meanings at different moments for different communities.

What do I mean by "different meanings"? A given object in a collection—a plant, for example—has a different meaning or significance to the botanist, to the ethno-botanist, the people who live[d] with it, the animals that live[d] with it, the zoologist, the landscape painter, the gardener, or the tourist. Each of these individuals brings his/her own worldview, with its rules, norms, and standards, to the perception of and interaction with the plant. Any one of the museums involved in the Urban Network might employ an expert from any one of the disciplines named above and therefore ascribe specific meaning to the plant in the collection. The educators writing in this book are developing new meanings for the plant when they successfully connect the plant with a community that uses its own ecological, historical, anthropological, theoretical, or disciplinary lens to consider the plant. This approach, while not ubiquitous, represents a significant shift in the museum's educative role and cultural relevance.

It is interesting to note that schools are undergoing a parallel process of examining their function as relevant educative institutions. For example, for decades school science has been taught as a collection of disparate facts and theories—all necessary building blocks for future scientists, but not all clearly relevant or usable for the other 99.9 percent of the student population. Current science education reform calls for rethinking the curriculum to promote science literacy for all students (NRC 1996; AAAS 1989). Science literacy means many different things, but includes an understanding of the nature of science, scientific ways of thinking, and methods of scientific inquiry. An ability to read and make sense of competing scientific views (as reported by the media) appears increasingly essential for active participation in many key political and ethical questions of today. Schools (and museums) also strive to provide more specialized knowledge for future scientists or enthusiasts, but today it is not an "either/or" but rather a "both/and" situation. Just as we all need to read but only some will become writers, we all need to understand the nature of science though only some will become physicists.

In the shift away from the transmission of a collection of scientific facts and theories to the development of scientific literacy, schools are seeking to incorporate many ways of teaching and learning that have long been espoused by interactive science museums like the Exploratorium. Teachers are attempting to integrate more learner-driven approaches to science teaching; they are using scientific argumentation and discourse as a way to develop scientific ways of thinking. New science education standards ask teachers to implement science inquiry and hands-on investigations in their classrooms. Because few in the school system were themselves educated in this way, schools are now turning to the museum field in increasing numbers to help make this transition to more inclusive (and constructivist) ways of teaching science.

The formal education system is an important (albeit large and sometimes daunting) community for the museum field to work with. It is important not only for bringing young people through our doors—to introduce them to the beauty and profundity of our collections and work—as we have done for 100 years already, but also for supporting an evolving worldview about the nature of subject-matter knowledge.

Sticking to my own museum's domain, the science museum can provide teachers with a window into the nature of science and the processes of scientific inquiry. It can support excellent science teachers, shoring up their content understanding, providing curricular and pedagogical resources, and developing innovative strategies for engaging their students with the subject matter. Museums can also support the many science teachers who have almost no science background or education (more than 30 percent of science teachers are teaching out of their field) by providing welcoming, non-didactic approaches to science that build on the teachers' questions and curiosity to draw them into the curricular domains of science. I believe this is true in other subject areas as well—historical inquiry in a museum, literary inquiry, sociology and art.

The challenge before the museum field is to resist distorting the museum experience into a Carnegie unit of 50 minutes of instruction. In many cases, even hands-on activities can be quite didactic—leading students through a series of steps toward a prescribed endpoint. The museum experience ideally allows any visitor—with any given level of prior experience with the subject matter—to enter the environment, walk towards what appeals, and spend as much time as desired engaged with the exhibit. Visitors can glance up and find related objects or texts and be drawn on to deeper understanding by engaging with one of a range of exhibits placed in proximity. Each visitor leaves the museum with a changed understanding based on what they knew, their ways of constructing knowledge, and the facilitation or mediation provided by the museum.

In embracing the school community in particular, museums need to build on what they know about learning—as reflected in their exhibition and mediation designs. Learning is contextually based, constructed through social discourse, and built upon iterative experiences with subject matter. Museums also need to attend to what schools can teach them about cognitive development and children. At a time when the cognitive sciences are dramatically influencing the way schools think about structuring teaching and learning, museums are in a strong position to support both teachers and students in the development of subject-matter knowledge, the nature and epistemology of the subject matter (whether physics, archaeology, anthropology, or the fine arts), and pedagogical content knowledge.

No matter which community the museums work with, the shift we seem to be describing in this book is one away from being connoisseurs and brokers of a fixed body of knowledge toward coming to understand a collection in relationship to a range of needs, perceptions, and resources extant beyond the museum walls.

The window that museums provide is not a one-way or even a two-way window. Different worlds look in, sometimes at the same time, and they see differ- ent things. The art of the educative role of museums is in linking their unique resources and knowledge to a variety of communities whose inquiries and experience become richer, deeper, and more engaging because of what the museum has brought to bear on the world of the perceiver. And the museum needs to build on what it learns from its partners to constantly renew and replenish itself, remaining current, relevant, and integrated into the web of knowledge that defines, embraces, and emanates from society.

Works Cited

American Association for the Advancement of Science (AAAS). 1989. *Science for All Americans: A Project 2061 Report on Literacy Goals in Science, Mathematics, and Technology.* Washington, D.C.: American Association for the Advancement of Science.
Hein, G. 1998. *Learning in the Museum.* London: Routledge.
National Research Council (NRC). 1996. *National Science Education Standards.* Washington, D.C.: National Academy Press.
National Research Council (NRC). 2000. *How People Learn: Brain, Mind, Experience, and School.* Washington, D.C.: National Academy Press.
Vygotsky, L.S. 1978. *Mind in Society: The Development of Higher Psychological Processes.* Ed. M. Cole, et. al. Cambridge, Mass.: Harvard University Press.

Bronwyn Bevan is Director, Center for Informal Learning and Schools, Exploratorium.

Urban Network in Context

Ellen Wahl

My work has always been about promoting access and equity. But most of the time I have been outside, banging on the door, asking for resources. When I moved from working in community and youth organizations to the American Museum of Natural History, I stepped over the threshold. I found myself in the middle of a treasure trove of accumulated knowledge and dynamic research, beautiful objects that tell the story of human culture, specimens that are a record of life on earth, technologies that reveal our genetic origins and the beginnings of our universe, and hundreds of living human animals with expertise, talents, and connections.

When I was hired, Myles Gordon, my boss and the Vice President for Education, said that a large part of his job is "to give this place away," to see to it that a broad and diverse audience has a sense of comfort, belonging, and ownership in relation to the institution. The vision was to extend the museum beyond its walls and make it available especially to those whose resources and opportunities had been limited. My job here is a continuation of my life's work, but I feel a heightened sense of responsibility to get these incredible resources out the door to where I used to be, to *all* the publics, not just the subset that has always been comfortable and felt welcomed here.

All of the members of the Urban Network share this commitment to making the resources and collections of museums more available to more and different kinds of people. We join many others in rethinking the role of museums in society, in using the power of these influential institutions to shape and reflect knowledge, culture, and learning to include those who have not been included before.

A very brief and incomplete history of these efforts in the museum and related fields harkens back to the mid-1980s, when two of the key associations in the museum field, the American Association of Museums (AAM) and the Association of Science-Technology Centers (ASTC), laid the foundation for action to enhance diversity and expand outreach among their member organizations. AAM's 1984 report, *Museums for a New Century*, focused on the themes of public service and education, and its 1992 *Equity and Excellence* publication became a touchstone for the field. The AAM board elevated its diversity coalition to an administrative committee of the board in 2001. A national Museums and Community Initiative was established by AAM in 1998 "to explore the potential for renewed, dynamic engagement between museums and communities." A national task force, six community dialogues, and conversations with community and museum leaders led to a series of products and strategies, including *Mastering Civic Engagement: A Challenge to Museums*, a policy statement "designed to challenge museums to rethink their relationships with communities."

In 1985 ASTC began surveying its member organizations to determine who, in fact, was serving in positions of leadership. Armed with data that presented a monochromatic picture, ASTC launched a major initiative, Project MOSAIC, to diversify its representation. It brokered partnerships between science centers and community-based organizations with seed grants to invent new ways to work together. And it established a long-term youth initiative called YouthAlive! that funneled millions of dollars to museums across the country to support existing programs as well as to create new ones that would provide meaningful roles for youth, with a focus on urban, minority, and underserved youth. YouthAlive! was intended to open up museums in new ways and recognize young people as legitimate contributors; it also aimed to diversify both who served and who was served.

In both the art and science communities, these initiatives were part of movements to challenge notions about who can create, participate, and benefit from artistic or scientific ventures. Despite the fact that art is a fundamental component of human society, represented across every culture as well as in the fossil record of our hominid ancestors, many communities have been separated from doing, understanding, and appreciating art. Cutbacks in funding, limited public support, and attempts by governmental entities to legislate about what is acceptable art for public consumption have threatened core values of the freedom of expression.

Through the 1960s, science education was explicitly designed as a sorting mechanism, with only a small percentage of students continuing beyond eighth grade science, and most of these, because of differential access and stereotypes, were white males. By the early 1980s, it was clear that the United States could ill afford to continue keeping people out of science, and that it needed both the numbers as well as the diversity of talent if the country was to remain technologically competitive. The combination of a severe scientific workforce shortage and the need for a scientifically literate public led Congress to require the National Science Foundation (NSF) to redress the underrepresentation of women, minorities, and persons with disabilities in scientific and engineering education and careers (42 U.S.C. § 1885C). Beyond preparing the next generation of scientists and protecting the health of science (NSF's mission), NSF recognized that public understanding of science is essential to protecting the planet, the biodiversity of species, and the universe beyond.

- Everyone needs access to the tools and products of art.
- Everyone needs access to the knowledge and skills of science.
- A democratic nation depends on an informed and literate populace that values freedom of expression.
- A sustainable planet depends on communities of humans that can reflect on and take responsibility for their actions.

So here we Urban Network members sit, in these places of knowledge and beauty. We see barriers that keep people away—tangible barriers, like transportation and cost of admission—and intangible barriers—like feeling unwelcome, intimidated, or irrelevant. We wrestle with how to take these barriers down, how to get our "stuff" out to communities who can't or don't come in, how to say to folks in words and actions that you are wanted and valued here. We try to figure out what approaches to change will work, how we learn from and build on past efforts, and how we join together to aggregate our individual acts into powerful movements.

The case studies in this book offer new solutions to old problems, and time-honored answers to new challenges. They demonstrate that there are many ways to effect change in how museums carry out their missions of public service and education, how they share and redistribute their resources, how they serve their publics and join with their communities—in every sense of the word. This book is an attempt to capture some good ideas and to inspire others to join us.

Ellen Wahl is Director of Youth, Family, and Community Programs at American Museum of Natural History.

Making a Way Outta No Way: Lessons I've Learned from Our Diversity Project Community Partners

Patricia Williams Lessane

Through a generous grant from the National Recreation Foundation, The Field Museum's Diversity Project has afforded more than 1,000 children and their parents from some of Chicago's most marginalized communities the opportunity to view Field Museum special exhibitions and attend lectures, festivals, workshops, and summer camp. This same grant has given me the opportunity to advocate for these communities and learn invaluable life lessons about what civic duty and "giving back" truly mean.

The progeny of parents who migrated from the segregated South during the 1940s, I grew up learning about the geographic lines that demarcate the "city of big shoulders" and determine where the "haves" and "have-nots" live. While my parents had little formal education, they were community-minded, great storytellers, and blessed with the gift of listening. Having fearless parents who stepped beyond the racial division lines to embrace people regardless of race, ethnicity, or class taught me to listen to the stories, dreams, and struggles of our diverse community partners and helped me enter into their lives.

When I was offered the position of Diversity Project Administrator, I was thrilled to have the chance to help people *from my community* get involved with The Field Museum's wonderful and innovative programs. My job is to develop and nurture partnerships with community organizations, social service agencies, churches, and schools from the surrounding neighborhoods that enrich the museum experiences of their constituents and give us invaluable information about how they perceive and experience The Field Museum. Our partners get free museum admission and we use what we learn from them to create museum experiences that are welcoming to all visitors.

Melding my fervor for community advocacy with my love for The Field Museum seemed like a dream come true. And in many ways it has been. I have taken the history, reputation, and programs of The Field Museum into neighborhoods, churches, homes, and lives of people from all walks of life. I enjoy marketing Field Museum programs to people who might otherwise not know about these educational opportunities or be able to afford them. In doing so, I have learned that audience diversity is not that difficult to achieve—success lies in truly *listening* to what our partner organizations say about what they want and need and in the sincerity of "the ask" for partnership. When we ask an organization to participate in the Diversity Project, we are asking them not only to visit and take part in museum programs, but also to speak openly and honestly about their experiences when they come so that we can learn what programs attract them and what they expect from us as a civic institution.

Implementing suggestions from their feedback leads to another lesson: the desire to broaden a museum's audience must be institution-wide, not just the goal of one department or division. Only when an honest and balanced approach to partnership is thoughtfully conveyed can real partnerships be born.

As an African-American woman, educator, researcher, and native Chicagoan, my experience as "other" has helped me in my endeavors to make "others" become and feel a part of The Field Museum community. My historical membership in one of the surrounding communities of color has, in my mind, yielded the Diversity Project its greatest rewards. Early on, potential community partners in Black and Latino neighborhoods often said, "I'm glad you're there. How did that happen?" suggesting a relief, happiness, and disbelief that a Black person had been hired to bring poor, black, brown, immigrant, and non-English speaking people into The Field Museum. With pride and a little of my own disbelief, I would answer, "I'm glad I'm here too." That's how many of our most fulfilling partnerships were born. I began simply by calling and visiting agencies I knew or learned of through referrals. I'd tell them about the initiative to broaden the museum's audience, ask them about the educational or cultural programs they offered their clients, and whether they would like The Field Museum to help provide "edutaining" outlets for their communities. I never encountered an agency, church, or organization that turned down the opportunity to partner with us.

But the road to diversity has been riddled with funding potholes and allocation loopholes on both sides. Our inability to provide transportation to or food at our events for many of our community organizations during the first year made it difficult for some to participate, because their constituents rely on them for meals and transportation to programs and field trips. Many of our partners struggle with limited staff and resources.

We have learned that lack of transportation is one of the greatest barriers impeding many of the people we are trying to reach from taking advantage of all we offer. We have begun to offer bus transportation and transit cards to help our community partners get their constituents to our programs. The results have been great. We saw an increase in attendance at our temporary exhibitions in the summer, the Cultural Connection Kick-Off event this fall, and the Women's Board holiday party.

During our first year, I half joked with Beth Crownover, Manager of Public Programs, that our motto should be "expect the unexpected" because the community partner participation was often much higher, and in some cases, lower than we expected. For example, during "Summer World Tour 2001," our summer camp program with the Adler Planetarium and The Shedd Aquarium, I allocated 30 slots for the Better Boys Foundation (BBF), per their request. When we had not received all of their permission slips or participants' names by the extended deadline, we informed them that we would give away the remaining slots. However, on the first day of camp, we were met bright and early by not 30, but 35 smiling children from BBF! Since we could not accommodate them all, we made provisions for the unexpected children to spend the day at The Field Museum and to participate in off-site activities the next day.

When I spoke with Darlene Boyd, Director of Educational Outreach at BBF, about the confusion, she said, "Patricia, if you give me 30 slots, I'm gonna fill them. It might take me up until the last minute, but I'll fill them. I'm trying hard to expose these children to as many educational and cultural programs as possible. They need so much and we have so little. So bear with me." I did bear with her and "her children" frequented the museum several times for overnights, the holiday party, summer camp, and to see the "Chocolate" exhibition.

Darlene exemplifies the drive, dedication, and insight our community partners bring to the Diversity Project. And it is very clear to her and our other partners that diversifying The Field Museum not only helps their constituents, but also The Field Museum. "The Field Museum can't expect us to come to the museum and increase the number of people of color who visit the museum, without once coming to our community. That's not giving back," she said. Other partners have echoed the same desire for The Field Museum to do its civic duty to surrounding communities by bringing educational and cultural programming directly into their neighborhoods.

On one of my first visits to New Phoenix Assistance Center on the South Side, Case Manager Inita Powell said, "Patricia, we will come to whatever you invite us to. I will bring my entire roster of clients and their children—we want to explore the museum. But we need The Field Museum all year long. Can you bring some activities, books, and snacks out to our site? That's what we need. We'll help you, but can you help us?"

We listened to Inita. We realized we could do more and we have begun to do just that. For example, we now offer off-site follow-up workshops for partners on the content of the exhibitions seen on their visits to enhance their educational experience. A generous grant from Kraft also allowed us to give books and puzzles to children who saw "Chocolate," "Sue," and the "Tiniest Giants" exhibitions.

Inita and her clients are now regulars at the museum and are comfortable with making requests about what they would like to see at the museum or explaining why they especially liked or disliked a program. For an upcoming overnight, Inita lobbied all summer and succeeded in getting 40 sleeping bags donated by a local store to the families attending. She often says she knows how to "make a way out of no way," an African-American saying that means making what seems impossible happen.

Inita's courage and ability to make things happen for her clients is reflective of all of our partners. Another example of creativity, tenacity, and diversity comes from one of our partners in Chicago Roger's Park community.

North Point Advancement Center is a fledgling community center, housed in a low-income housing development, which offers programs for children, teens, and seniors. The participants are primarily African American, Mexican, Puerto Rican, and African. Selena Awoleye, the Director, has a miniscule budget and only one staff person, but she has managed to offer chess lessons, soccer, arts and crafts, and Girls Scouts by using the human resources around her. The chess instructor is her mailman and the soccer coach is the maintenance man—who secured for the mostly African-American team donated uniforms in the official colors of Mexico!

Listening to her stories fills me with a sense of pride about the people I work with and whose lives I get to help enrich in a small way. It also gives me hope because if Selena can impact lives with her limited resources, we at The Field Museum definitely can make an impact.

Our community partners constantly have to make their limited funding dollars stretch to meet the demands of the masses they serve. They look at us—a gargantuan institution with our spectacular exhibitions and state funding—and think that if they can make a way out of no way with the little they have, then surely we can do even more.

They are right. Museum educators and administrators alike must learn the art of making a way out of no way. In these times of scarce funding for programs serving minorities, people of color, and poor people, it is a necessity. As civic and cultural institutions, it is our responsibility.

We must listen more attentively to the needs and ideas of the people we want to help and value what they have to say and offer us as an institution. If we want real partnerships with organizations that reflect the diversity of this great city, we must take resources into their communities, just as their presence in our museum enriches us. When we sincerely extend ourselves to our community partners and use what we learn to enrich the lives of all visitors, then we are truly "giving back" to all people.

The survival stories of our community partners are as colorful and diverse as the different people they serve, and they keep me excited about my work. These are a few of the invaluable lessons I have learned from them.

Patricia Williams Lessane is Diversity Project Administrator at The Field Museum.

Section 3
Program Development Blueprint

Program Development Blueprint

This guide to program development evolved out of conversations among Urban Network members, a group of seasoned museum practitioners who plan and implement innovative programs that build relationships between diverse communities and museums. In talking about what we do in our work, we took a step back to reflect upon our practice and break apart the steps we take, sometimes instinctively, to plan and implement these programs. By comparing stories, analyzing our practices, and sharing our own lessons learned from successes and failures, we came up with the following guidelines for building programs that engage diverse communities.

While each new initiative we plan may be unique to us, surveying the field to learn what others have done with a similar challenge can be a useful and enlightening way to begin. Scanning the local cultural scene to see what other institutions have tried in our own cities and towns can be especially instructive. Don't be afraid to pick up the phone. Our experience in Urban Network has taught us how much we can learn from one another and how eager we all are to talk about our experiences.

We recognize that each program or initiative exists within the larger context of our institutions' ongoing commitment to increasing access to museum learning. Each program, whether catalyzed by a single exhibition or organized as a long-term initiative, advances our institution's efforts to provide better service to an increasingly diverse public.

Among a museum's many constituents and stakeholders, each new program will have its own set of initial allies and those who are hesitant and need to be cultivated. Much of our conversation focused around gaining support and building relationships both within our institutions and within our neighboring communities.

This blueprint is organized by the questions we ask ourselves when planning new initiatives and the kinds of information we seek when attempting to answer these questions in our own practice. The colored pages provide reference tools to help you envision a program and how it can impact your institution's goals towards civic engagement, build healthy partnerships and advisory committees, and take practical steps to collaborative program development.

Context for Program Planning

When we set out to help museums "embrace communities," we are trying to bring about change in "who forms, informs, and benefits from" these influential institutions (Jolly 2002). There are several preliminary steps that can help to define the task and set the context for program development:

Figure 1

Questions to Ask About Key Relationships When Planning a New Civic Engagement Program

(P) Primary Relationships

1 Program Participants to Program

- Who are the target audiences that will benefit?
- What are the program goals?
- How will the program fulfill the participants' needs?
- How should the participants be involved in the program development and implementation?
- How will the participants learn about the program?
- What will motivate them to participate?
- What will bring them back again and again?
- What are the checkpoints to examine program progress and any necessary adjustments?

2 Institution to Program

- How does this program fit within the museum's mission, goals, and priorities?
- How will you involve colleagues in the development of the program? How will they benefit?
- Which colleagues will be involved in implementing the program and how will they be involved in planning?
- How can the lessons learned from this program inform practice throughout the museum?
- To what extent is the museum committed to sustaining the impact of this program?

3 External Stakeholders to Program
(External stakeholders include collaborators, cooperators, partners, funders, government, etc.)

- Which external stakeholders will the program impact?
- How will they be involved in program planning and implementation?
- How will the program address their needs and expectations?

(S) Secondary Relationships

4 Institution to External Stakeholders

- What is the desired impact of this program or initiative on the long-term relationship between the institution and the external stakeholders?
- Can the benefits of this experience be leveraged to make gains in other areas?
- How will the program components and results be communicated?

5 Institution to Program Participants

- What are the goals for the museum with this audience beyond this program or initiative?
- Can the museum parlay a positive experience into a more sustained benefit for the institution? If so, how?
- Who needs to be involved in the planning and/or communication loop to make this happen?

6 Program Participants to External Stakeholders

- What are the external stakeholders' goals for building relationships with program participants through this initiative?
- How are these addressed in the program planning?

- Define what you are trying to change—who, what, where, and why. For example, are your visitors reflective of your surrounding communities? If not, why not? Has your institution recently made an assessment of its commitment to civic engagement as it strives to serve its mission and goals?

- Conduct a review of the field—who else has done anything similar, locally, nationally, or internationally? What does the literature say about viable strategies, what do we know from the research base about what works for whom and under what conditions? What is salient for you to consider as you plan, what is transferable to your situation, what are the potential pitfalls based on others' experience?

- Identify your "theory of change" or framework for action. What's your causal model: if I do *(a)*, then I think *(b)* will happen and *(c)* will be different as a result? (For example, cutting admission price and advertising in lower-income communities will increase numbers of visitors from those communities.) Will you involve the powers-that-be at the outset and try to change policy and the way the institution does business? Or will you "just do it" and demonstrate from the bottom up that things can be done differently?

The questions in Figure 1 focus on relationships between different groups of people inside and outside the museum. The questions may help you to identify "who forms, informs, and benefits," to describe the landscape as you begin, and to see the mountains (or hills!) you may have to move to achieve your results.

Institutional Self-Assessment

? How could this initiative further the goals and mission of the institution?

No matter how creative and inventive the idea, implementing it requires the commitment of a broad range of constituents inside and outside of the museum. To earn support, the program must clearly help the museum fulfill its mission and priorities and it must address a genuine need in the community.

When identifying allies, think about internal constituencies such as museum management, trustees or board members, colleagues, volunteer groups, and content specialists within the museum. Also, consider external constituents such as community organizations, funders, the media, arts and cultural organizations, political leaders, and other potential collaborators. While planning your program, think about how and when to include each of the stakeholders and how you will communicate with them throughout the program cycle (Rand 2001).

? How do you build momentum behind a program within the museum?

When making a case to gain support for a program within the museum, it may be helpful to present the program in terms of costs versus benefits. All programs,

Figure 2　**SWOT Example**

Strengths (internal)	Opportunities (external)
• Staff expertise	• Upcoming exhibition/program
• Collections/exhibitions	• Interested public
• Funding	• Enthusiastic funder
	• Supportive local government

Weaknesses (internal)	Threats (external)
• Lack of diversity within the institution	• Negative perception of the institution
• Lack of institutional commitment	• Language/cultural barriers
• Lack of diversity within the collections	• Competition
• Lack of experience/knowledge	• Physical and intellectual inaccessibility

Figure 3　**Factors to Consider in Developing Audience Advisory Groups**

- What is the role of the group? Should it be project-specific or ongoing?

- What department should lead the effort? Will it have interdepartmental implications?

- How much staff time will be needed to maintain the group? How much is available?

- Who will oversee the group? What criteria should be considered in choosing the museum representative? This selection carries significance, e.g., key staff leader with interdepartmental authority or line staff person, person of similar descent or not.

- Who will identify and select the members of the group?

- How often will the group meet? (quarterly, monthly)

- What will the group discuss? Who will set the agenda?

even those that are completely funded with grant money, require an institutional investment of staff, management time, and institutional resources—all resources that would be devoted to *this* initiative and *not* something else. The benefit to the museum is measured by how well the initiative fulfills the museum's mission, goals and priorities, and the needs of the community. To build internal support, consider how different museum departments or functions will benefit from the program. Articulating and understanding the costs and benefits of a program helps to initiate conversations that build support for it and to anticipate objections. Also, it helps the museum and its collaborators to consider their commitment to sustaining the impact of the program over time.

(?) **How would this program fit within the broader context of the museum's past and present initiatives?**

Does it dovetail with another initiative? Build on prior experience? Can it be leveraged into a larger initiative? Can it serve as a model for working with other communities? Or is it a first-time effort in a brand new field? One decision an institution may face, especially in tight economic times, is breadth or depth. How many relationships can the museum afford to sustain at one time? Should it continue to maintain an ongoing relationship with one community, or reach out to build new relationships with other communities? The overall context of a strategic plan can help inform these decisions.

(?) **How do you organize a self-assessment inquiry?**

Once the idea is formulated and reasonably supported, many museums find it useful to organize a self-assessment inquiry through a SWOT analysis. SWOT stands for Strengths, Weaknesses, Opportunities, and Threats. In general, strengths and weaknesses assess internal museum factors, while opportunities and threats look at external factors that may impact the success of the initiative. The SWOT analysis helps to determine whether the proposed program is a good fit for the institution and to identify areas to address during program planning.

Some museums have found that conducting a SWOT analysis in a meeting with all the museum departments who would be involved in executing the program is an effective strategy to strengthen the program concept, build relationships within the museum, and gain support from key department staff and management. See Figure 2 for an example of the types of information that might be considered in the different categories of a SWOT analysis.

Audience Assessment

"If you build it, they will come" might attract the ghosts of dead baseball players in the movies, but it does not work well for engaging new audiences in museums. Once the museum identifies which audience it wishes to reach with an initiative, the next step is to identify the assets within that community that could contribute to the initiative and the motivating factors for this audience to participate. The best way to learn this is from the target audiences themselves.

? How do you learn about the community?

When researching a potential audience, recognize that every community is diverse and talk with as many people representing different perspectives as you can. Ask for their advice about which organizations you might partner or collaborate with on initiatives. Meet the representatives of these organizations and, most importantly, listen.

As museums we need to recognize that we can be viewed by the community as very "mysterious" places. Consider what can be done to demystify the museum and make it more accessible to a broader community. In addition to preparing your own questions, try to anticipate the community's questions and be prepared for an open, honest exchange of ideas and information. Forming an advisory committee might be helpful (see Figure 3). The Oakland Museum's case study in this book offers a good illustration of the important role an advisory committee can play in influencing the museum's programming and collections.

What is your history with this audience? ?

If your museum has been around for a while, chances are there is a history with the audience you are researching. Always begin by asking around the museum to see whether anyone, in any of the departments, is currently working with this community or knows of a prior relationship between the museum and this community. If you do uncover something, try to find out all you can about it, especially whether it was a positive or negative experience. Colleagues with long institutional memories are very valuable. Identify whom museum colleagues already know from that community and try to build upon existing relationships.

? How does this initiative benefit the community?

We find that looking at communities that are traditionally "underserved" through the lens of what exists instead of what does not can open the doors to whole new worlds of possibility. Every community has assets—community, civic, religious, cultural, social service, arts, or sports organizations; the traditions, languages, and histories of the people and groups who were born or immigrated there; schools, colleges, trade schools, and other places of formal learning; parks, playgrounds, libraries, zoos, historical societies, or museums; elders and other local wise people; community events and celebrations (Kretzmann et. al. 1997). Each asset represents an opportunity for the museum to learn from the community and to understand how it can offer something that the community needs. It is a community's assets, not its needs or deficits, that illuminate gateways for the museum to engage with that community.

Just as a program has to make sense for the museum, it needs to fulfill the mission of partner organizations too. A SWOT analysis from the community partner's perspective can provide useful information. Pinpointing and articulating program objectives and sharing information about costs and budgets helps to assure that everyone is on the same page and in clear agreement about intended outcomes. The initiative will provide reciprocal benefit to each of the right community partners.

It is important to note that there are varying levels of participation by community organizations (see Figure 4). They range from serving as advisors, to cooperating to support a program, to coordinating efforts between institutions, to full collaboration and partnership requiring a deep commitment and a certain level of risk from the community. It is important to match the level of involvement by the community organization with the degree it can commit resources to the endeavor.

Relationship Building

? **How do you begin a relationship with community partners?**

Treat every relationship with respect and dignify everyone with the kind of care you would give if meeting your new in-laws for the first time. Recognize that you may be coming from very different cultures, literally and figuratively, with different norms, values, and ways of doing things. You may need to become anthropologists in each others' lands.

There are no short-term, quick-fix relationships of convenience. Communities have long memories and being dismissive or treating someone disrespectfully can bring long-term negative consequences and hamper the museum's future initiatives to connect with this community.

Sample Agenda for an Initial Planning Meeting with Community Partner Organizations

Part I: Assessment

- What are the commonalities between our organizations' missions?
- What values do we share?
- What goals do we share?
- What are our differences?
- How does each organization prioritize these shared goals?
- What challenges do we each face now?

Part II: Exploration and Planning

- Suggest a specific potential program or collaborative initiative.
- Listen to responses and concerns, gauge interest/enthusiasm.
- Emphasize that the idea is at an early stage and needs their input.
- Brainstorm together about how to develop the idea (or brainstorm about other possible collaborations given the information yielded in Part I and then develop the best one).

Figure 4   **Levels of Engagement**

Cooperation is characterized by informal relationships that exist without any commonly defined mission, structure, or planning effort. Information is shared as needed, and authority is retained by each organization so there is virtually no risk. Resources are separate, as are rewards.

Coordination is characterized by more formal relationships and understanding of compatible missions. Some planning and division of roles are required, and communication channels are established. Authority still rests with the individual organizations, but there is some increased risk to all participants. Resources are available to participants and rewards are mutually acknowledged.

Collaboration connotes a more durable and pervasive relationship. Collaborations bring previously separate organizations into a new structure with full commitment to a common mission. Such relationships require comprehensive planning and well-defined communication channels operating on many levels. Authority is determined by the collaborative structure. Risk is much greater because each member of the collaboration contributes its own resources and reputation. Resources are pooled or jointly secured, and the products are shared.

(These definitions have been adapted from *Collaboration: What Makes it Work*, published by the Amherst H. Wilder Foundation, 1992, St. Paul, Minn.)

Figure 5   **Twelve Ingredients for Building Healthy Partnerships**

These principles apply whether collaborating on a single exhibit or developing a long-term program.
- Put time and energy into building trust.
- Set specific and clear expectations.
- Define what roles each partner will play.
- Define each partner's responsibilities.
- Develop and agree upon a clear decision-making process.
- Establish mutually agreeable avenues of communication.
- Set up critical review points to discuss intermediate progress.
- Be willing to adapt or revisit programs, procedures or policies so that the museum can better meet the needs of the community and truly collaborate.
- Discuss who will handle money.
- Determine who will be responsible for documenting the program and how it will be done.
- Agree upon goals and methods for evaluating whether goals are achieved.
- Determine whether aspects of the agreement need to be solidified in writing and don't be afraid to do so.

Be aware that some partnerships are not created equal. The museum may be an imposing and seemingly "rich" institution that was established to reflect and sustain the dominant culture, while the community partner may be operating on a shoestring budget and committed to change in the social order.

Sometimes it helps to acknowledge the imbalance, sometimes it's best left unspoken. Either way, recognizing what each stands to gain from the connection can make it easier to define a shared agenda and to affirm the reciprocal nature of the relationship. Building trust begins with attentive listening, being open to change, responding, and being honest and straightforward. It is very important to take feedback and constructive criticism very seriously (with some degree of humor) by viewing them as opportunities for assessing museum procedures or policies that might create obstacles. If a partner's suggestions cannot be addressed, explaining why will help to build the partner's understanding of the museum. To avoid misleading community partners, museum representatives should tell community partners at the outset the extent that the museum is committed to sustaining the program.

In addition to defining the parameters of the project and the partnership agreement, it is useful to discuss and understand each organization's limitations. A discussion about priorities often helps to clarify some of these issues. Sometimes partners may share their top two or three priorities, but assign different values to them. It is important to understand what is in each partner's interest and what would be a "deal-breaker" for each.

Also consider how each organization will address or serve the increased interest or requests from the community generated through this program. An institutional mechanism or commitment needs to be in place to respond to these requests in order to build the relationship that is so needed for sustaining networks and collaborations (see Figure 5).

(**?**) **How can your community partners help you build relationships with community members?**

Community partners that already have relationships with and the trust of the target audience can be helpful in delivering the marketing message to the target audience and in providing "safe" avenues of access for community members to the museum. The Science Museum of Minnesota's case study in this book is an excellent example of partnerships set up expressly for this purpose. Assessing marketing and outreach strategies with the community partners early and often can help direct marketing resources to the most fruitful avenues.

Figure 6

Museums and Community Collaboration: Ten Steps to Successful Program Development

Step 1

Define the educational philosophy or rationale for the program.

Step 2

Set specific goals in terms of:
- Audience numbers
- Timelines
- Demographics
- Learning outcomes
- Products, i.e., curriculum, exhibition, Web site, etc.

Step 3

Describe exactly what the program is in 50 to 100 words. State the purpose of the program and answer "we do what, for whom, and for what outcome/benefit?"

Step 4

Define program specifics, such as:
- Where it takes place
- When it takes place
- Who does it and what they do
- How resources will be shared

Step 5

Inventory resources, including:
- Museum staff expertise (curatorial/ research content, education, and administrative)
- Teaching materials
- Budget for the program
- Staff expertise and resources for each partner organization
- Spaces and equipment
- Current and potential funding sources
- Additional staff, teaching materials, or other resources and funding needed to fill in gaps in existing resources

Step 6

Work with community collaborators/ partners to:
- Research community to identify and recruit advisors, collaborators, or partners.
- Clarify roles and responsibilities for community involvement based on available resources and shared goals and priorities.
- Establish process for timely communications and decision-making.

- Consider forming an advisory committee to help support the endeavor.

Step 7

Market the program.
- Solicit feedback from representatives of the targeted community regarding marketing strategies, messages, and materials.
- Name the program.
- Choose a variety of marketing and media strategies.
- Create visually attractive materials (postcards, posters, etc.) that community members will want to distribute to their constituents.
- Determine program fee (if there is one) that will match the "perceived value" of the program by the target audience.

Step 8

Determine documentation strategies.
- Who is responsible?
- What methods will be used?
- How will the documentation be used?
- Are additional funds required?

Step 9

Set a formative evaluation strategy.
- What are the critical checking-in points? Determine when and how often the program should be evaluated.
- How will the program be assessed? By whom?
- How will results be communicated to each set of stakeholders?
- What method and cycle will be used for making changes to improve the program?

Step 10

Set a summative evaluation strategy.
- How will the program be evaluated at its completion and by whom?
- How will progress towards goals be measured?
- How will the impact on each of the relationships in the program evaluation rubric be measured?
- How will results be communicated to stakeholders?

Program Development

Successful program development depends on having a good idea about what it is you want to do and have to offer. What is special about your museum that is worth sharing with others, and what is special about your potential partners that they can bring to the museum? What new product or value comes from joining your resources and areas of expertise? What is your shared vision of what will change for the museum and what will change for your partner? The ten steps outlined in Figure 6 may provide museums and communities with some guide posts for developing collaborative programs.

Sustaining Institutional Commitment of All Partners

Program development decisions and rationale will flow more readily once you have gained the commitment and clarity of purpose from self- and audience assessments. To the extent possible, all the collaborators should provide input and agree upon the program specifics, such as where and when it takes place, and exactly who does what. The museum will be rewarded if it can be flexible to meet internal and external partner and community needs. Making sure that everyone's expenses are acknowledged and covered by the budget also helps keep things running smoothly.

Creating checkpoints and feedback cycles within the project allows participants and all stakeholders to continually assess and improve the program. When planning, be sure to include time and resources for appropriate documentation. These feedback cycles—and the quality of the documentation fed into them—are important not only to fine-tune program strategies but also to acknowledge success. Success is something that can be and should be celebrated even when it is not complete.

By setting program goals and planning with collaborators, program planners lay the groundwork for evaluation. In addition to measuring progress towards quantitative goals, discuss which relationships will be most important to evaluate and how you will do it.

Operational Tips

Sometimes, even when all the groundwork is laid in terms of relationship building and planning, things happen within organizations or the environment that hamper progress or prevent synchronicity. Changes in key personnel, policy shifts that affect budget or mission priority, or mismatches in personality can threaten to derail good initiatives. While these circumstances are often unavoidable, try to maintain enough flexibility within the project so that you can discuss alternatives and change what you're doing. Being open to change is critical when working within a larger dynamic community. What can at first be perceived as unexpected crises can turn into new opportunities that often yield even better results. Strong partnerships built on a foundation of trust and respect are more likely to weather these challenges.

Works Cited

Kretzmann, John P., John L. McKnight, and Geralyn Sheehan. 1997. *A Guide to Capacity Inventories: Mobilizing the Community Skills of Local Residents*. Evanston, Ill.: Institute for Policy Research.

Jolly, Eric J. 2002. Confronting Demographic Denial: Retaining Relevance in the New Millennium. Washington, D.C.: *ASTC Dimensions* (January–February).

McCarthy, Kevin F., and Kimberly Jimmett. 2001. Appendix B: Survey results: participation-building activities. In *A New Framework for Building Participation in the Arts*. Santa Monica, Calif.: RAND Corporation.

Participants

Program Development Blueprint Discussion Group: Beth Crownover, Norma Dolcater, Robert Eskridge, Patricia Williams Lessane, Alisa Martin, Carolee Smith Rogers, Sarah Schultz, Sophia Siskel, Jean Sousa, Jennifer Amdur Spitz, Mary Ann Steiner

Additional Collaborators: Barbara Henry, Paul Mohrbacher, Ellen Wahl

Written By *Jennifer Amdur Spitz*

Section 4 Evaluation

Evaluation

The idea to build an evaluation rubric evolved from several discussions within Urban Network about "best practices" relative to audience engagement and a desire to work toward being able to define them. Before developing a new initiative, we all scan the field to glean ideas and lessons learned from others who went before us. As a consortium, we are rich because nearly all of us bring to Urban Network experiences from one or more of the other national audience diversity initiatives in the arts, sciences, or humanities. We know that none of us is inventing the wheel, but what more can we learn from one another and how can we frame our discussion in a way that brings us the most clarity about our practice?

The following evaluation rubric is the result of our attempt to set a framework for examining and discussing diverse audience engagement initiatives, especially those developed in community partnerships of all kinds. We designed this rubric to outline the types of questions we need to ask ourselves about the process as well as the products of audience engagement initiatives and to pinpoint the intersections where we are seeking change. We design and implement programs to engage diverse audiences upon a logic model that says if we affect *(a)*, then *(b)* is going to change and *(c)* will be different because of it. The questions in this rubric are designed to help evaluate if this logic is true and understand why or why not.

Advancing Mission, Meeting Needs

Successful community engagement programs are win-win in nature. They further the museum's mission while addressing community needs. Evaluating a program's alignment with mission and needs gets to the heart of a program's rationale, goals, and objectives. It encourages questions essential to a healthy relationship: Are all parties involved both giving to and receiving from the program in ways that are rewarding to them? Are the basic premises of the program well founded?

Relationship Changes

Most evaluations focus on assessing the relationship between the program and the participant, from either quantitative or qualitative perspectives. For example, who participated in the program and what did they derive from it? When Urban Network members began to consider the various elements of successful programming for community engagement, we agreed that two additional constituencies needed to be added to the evaluation mix—namely the institution (museum) sponsoring the program and any external stakeholders involved in it. Clearly, sustainable, community-based programs require both institutional and external stakeholder endorsement. As the dialogue proceeded, Urban Network participants concluded that the various constituencies should not only be measured for their relationships to the program, but also for their relationships to one another. Thus the group came up with the following evaluation rubric that identifies six sets of relationships associated with community engagement programs. Three relationships may be considered primary—they involve the program directly and are the ones that programming professionals are most likely to assess:

- Program participants to the program
- Institution (museum) to the program
- External stakeholders (including collaborators, cooperators, partners, funders, government) to the program

Three additional relationships may be considered secondary to the program—they are relationships that exist independently of the program but may be affected positively or negatively by the program. These relationships are often longer term and more mission-driven than those associated with individual programs. Though often neglected in evaluations, they are essential to programmatic success:

- Institution to external stakeholders
- Institution to program participants
- Program participants to external stakeholders

It is important to examine how relationships between groups or perceptions of one group by another have changed as a result of a program. The relationship between an institution and a community change according to the types of programs and level and frequency of interactions over time.

What Is the Evaluation Rubric?

Urban Network members created the evaluation rubric as a tool for museums to use to assess the efficacy of their community engagement programs in meeting program goals. It is also designed to help gauge the broader impact these programs have on the institutions and communities that support them. Although the rubric is comprehensive, it is also a work in progress. We offer it as a generic template that can be applied, tested, and refined to fit each program's unique circumstances.

Using the Rubric

The rubric is a complex and potentially daunting tool for programmers with limited time to evaluate their work. At the least, Urban Network participants hoped that by specifying the various relationships essential to successful community engagement, the rubric would spur other professionals to acknowledge the presence and evolution of these relationships in the course of program implementation. While we encourage those applying the rubric to give careful consideration to each of the questions posed, we recognize that different institutions and programs will benefit from placing greater emphasis on selected relationships and areas within them. In this respect, we hope that the rubric will be viewed as a flexible resource rather than a prescriptive form. In addition to using the rubric for formally evaluating a program, one can also use it informally as a reflective tool. During the process of developing the rubric, Urban Network members used the relationship-based questions to interview one another about their respective programs, and we found in these approximately half-hour conversations that both interviewers and interviewees gained insight into the mechanisms behind community engagement.

Lessons Learned

The lessons learned—by participants, community partners, museum staff, etc.—as a result of a program are valuable resources if they are "mined." Good evaluations strive to discover how to do it better the next time. It is important to remember to gather this information from all perspectives, document it, and apply it when planning the next program or the next cycle of the same program. Some programs conduct formative evaluations throughout their implementation and make adjustments accordingly. It is always good practice to keep notes on lessons learned in a central file so that they can inform future program development strategies.

Communication of Results

Sometimes a program has remarkable results, but few beyond the program know of them. Evaluations can provide programmers with substantial and compelling documentation that can help leverage additional support for the program and make a compelling case for new programs like it. Two things need to be considered along with the evaluation: a strategy for disseminating the results to each of the stakeholders, and a set of tools to communicate the results to them. Tools might include a written report, video, interactive media such as a CD-ROM or Web site, or oral presentations at board or community meetings.

Methods for Measurement

As explained above, the evaluation rubric focuses on exploring the different relationships associated with community-based programming. Although it is comprehensive with regard to specifying the relationships evaluated, the rubric does not provide comprehensive or scientific guidelines for measuring change in these relationships. The evaluation rubric suggests some methods for measurement that can be used for each type of questioning, such as surveys, focus groups, and interviews. We recognize that measurement will vary tremendously from institution to institution and from program to program, based on human and financial resources and other considerations. We simply hope the suggestions for measuring relationships prompt ideas about the means for doing so.

By *Jennifer Amdur Spitz* and *Margaret Thom*, Consultants to Urban Network, and *Joel Hoffman*, Vice Director for Education and Program Development, Brooklyn Museum of Art.

Evaluation Rubric

Urban Network members collaboratively created this evaluation rubric as a tool for museums to assess the efficacy of community engagement programs in meeting program goals, and to gauge the broader impact these programs have on the institutions and communities that support them.

Key Relationships

In this rubric, six relationships are considered:

1. Program participants to the program
2. Institution to the program
3. External stakeholders to the program (external stakeholders include collaborators, cooperators, partners, funders, government, etc.)
4. Institution to external stakeholders
5. Institution to program participants
6. Program participants to external stakeholders

The first three relationships directly involve the program. The second three may be affected by the program.

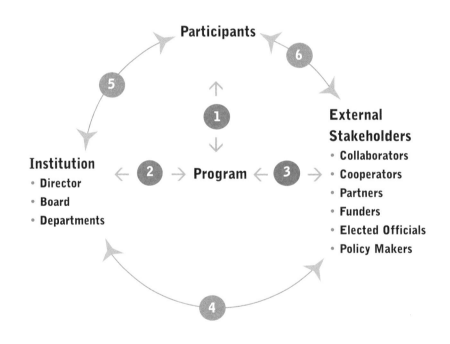

Key Questions

The rubric asks six questions as applied to these six relationships. The first three questions apply only to the primary three relationships. The second three questions apply to all six relationships.

	Primary Relationships			Secondary Relationships		
	1	**2**	**3**	**4**	**5**	**6**
	Program Participants to Program	Institution to Program	External Stakeholders to Program	Institution to External Stakeholders	Institution to Program Participants	Participants to External Stakeholders
A Who was served or engaged?						
				N/A	N/A	N/A
B Did the program fulfill the mission, values, or needs (as applicable)?						
				N/A	N/A	N/A
C Who was involved in program development and implementation and how?						
				N/A	N/A	N/A
D How did the program change relationships and perceptions?						
E What lessons were learned and what was/will be their impact?						
F How were program components/results communicated?						

Getting Started

To use this evaluation rubric, we suggest beginning with the following two items:

- Provide the name and a brief description of the program.
- Identify the program goals relative to community engagement.

Primary Relationships

Evaluating a Community Engagement Program's Effect on Its Primary Relationships

Below are suggested evaluation questions for the program's three primary relationships.

	Relationship 1: **Program Participants to Program**	Relationship 2: **Institution to Program**	Relationship 3: **External Stakeholders* to Program**
? A Who was served or engaged?			
	• Who composed the audience served? (Document quantity, age, gender, race, educational background, geography, etc.) • Were primary and secondary targets identified and assessed?	• Who was involved within your institution, including program staff and others?	• What external stakeholders were involved and at what level? *External stakeholders include collaborators, cooperators, partners, funders, government, etc.
? B Did the program fulfill the mission, values, or needs?			
	• Were the program's cognitive and/or affective goals met? • Did the program meet participants' needs? • Were there audience goals? If so, how did the audiences served compare to the program's targeted audience goals? • Were the needs of different ethnic/racial communities met? • For what reasons did the participants visit the institution?	• Did the program advance or impact the vision, mission, values, needs of your institution (relative to audience served, cognitive or affective behaviors, etc.)? If so, how?	• Did the program advance the vision, mission, values, needs of the external stakeholders (relative to audience served, cognitive or affective behaviors, etc.)? If so, how?
? C Who was involved in program development and implementation and how?			
	• Were program participants involved in the development of the program? If so, how did you select and involve them? • Did you shape the program based on participants' input? If so how? Was it ongoing?	• Outside of the program staff, were other colleagues at your institution involved in the development of the program? • If so, how did you select and involve them (supervisors, peers, board, etc.)? • Did you shape the program based on the input of other colleagues at your institution? If so, how? Was their input ongoing?	• Were external stakeholders involved in the development of the program? If so, how did you select and involve them? • Did you shape the program based on the input of external stakeholders? If so, how? Was their input ongoing?

Relationship 1: Program Participants to Program	Relationship 2: Institution to Program	Relationship 3: External Stakeholders* to Program

? D How did the program change relationships and perceptions?

• What were program participants' positive and negative perceptions of the program (include all program participants, primary and secondary)?	• Outside of the program staff, what were the positive and negative perceptions of the program among your institutional colleagues?	• What were external stakeholders' positive and negative perceptions of the program (include collaborators, cooperators, partners, funders, etc.)?

? E What lessons were learned and what was/will be their impact?

• What lessons were learned about participants' needs during program implementation? • How will these lessons inform future practice relative to this program (include marketing, cognitive or affective goals)?	• What did you learn about the institution's relationship to the program during program implementation? • Did your institution commit sufficient resources to achieve program goals? If not, please explain. • Based on lessons learned, have insights been incorporated into your institution's standard planning and operating procedures (e.g., fundraising)?	• What did you learn about stakeholder needs during program implementation? • How will lessons learned about stakeholder needs inform future practices related to this program?

Sect. IV
Evaluation

45

? F How were program components/results communicated?

• Was your marketing plan effective in attracting the desired participants (consider primary and secondary program participants)? What was most and least effective? • Did you share with your constituents your intent to evaluate the program and your willingness to modify the program based on their input?	• Did you invite appropriate parties within the museum (e.g., board, director, curators, etc.) to attend the program? If so, whom and how? • Did you effectively inform appropriate parties within the museum of program successes and challenges based on evaluation (this may include board reports, etc.)? If so, whom and how?	• Did you invite/inform appropriate external stakeholders to the program (including collaborators, cooperators, partners, funders, etc.)? If so, whom and how? • Did you apprise appropriate external stakeholders of program successes and challenges? If so, whom and how?

Methods for Measurement

Program Participants to Program

- Measure content and attitude change among program participants (using tests, surveys, and focus groups; document program participant baseline on content and attitude).
- Measure responsiveness of program to participants' performance/input (through evaluation of tests and surveys, evaluations as functions of sex, age, and ethnicity as appropriate).

Institution to Program

- Measure institutional change through awareness and support surveys (through focus groups).
- Measure institutional support of program (through anecdotal reports and questionnaires; document institutional baseline of performance expectations).

External Stakeholders to Program

- Measure stakeholders' expectations (through questionnaires, interviews).
- Measure stakeholders' impact on the program (anecdotal reports; document stakeholders' baseline for attitudes and expectations).

Secondary Relationships

Evaluating a Community Engagement Program's Effect on Its Secondary Relationships

Many program evaluations omit consideration of a program's secondary relationships, i.e., how it influences the relationships between the institution and external stakeholders, the institution and program participants, and program participants and external stakeholders. However, consideration of secondary relationships can yield important information and better assess the real impact and value of a community engagement program. Some suggested evaluation questions for these relationships follow.

Relationship 4: Institution to External Stakeholders	Relationship 5: Institution to Program Participants	Relationship 6: Program Participants to External Stakeholders

? D How did the program change relationships and perceptions?

• Did stakeholders' perceptions of the institution change as a result of the program? If so, how? • Did the institution's perception of the stakeholders change as a result of the program? If so, how? • Did the program cause increased communication between external stakeholders and the institution? If so, how?	• Did the program participants' perceptions of the institution change as a result of the program? If so, how? • Did the institution's perception of the program participants change as a result of the program? If so, how? • Did the program cause increased communication between program participants and the institution? If so, how?	• Did the program participants' perceptions of the stakeholders change as a result of the program? If so, how? • Did the stakeholders' perception of the program participants change as a result of the program? If so, how? • Did the program cause increased communication between external stakeholders and program participants? If so, how?

? E What lessons were learned and what was/will be their impact?

• What did you learn about the relationship between the museum and stakeholders during program implementation? • How will lessons learned from the program impact future relationships between the museum and stakeholders?	• What did you learn about the relationship between your institution and program participants during program implementation? • How will lessons learned from the program impact future relationships between your institution and program participants?	• What did you learn about the relationship between stakeholders and program participants during program implementation? • How will lessons learned from the program impact future relationships between stakeholders and program participants?

? F How were program components/results communicated?

• Did members of your institution outside of program staff communicate appropriate invitations to external stakeholders to participate in the program? If so, who invited whom and how? • Did external stakeholders communicate their enthusiasm or concerns for the program to members of your institution outside of program staff? If so, who communicated what to whom and how?	• Did members of the institution outside of program staff communicate appropriate invitations to participate in the program? If so, who invited whom and how? • Did program participants have opportunities to communicate their enthusiasm or concerns for the program to members of the institution outside of the program staff? If so, who communicated what to whom and how?	• Did external stakeholders use the program to reach their prospective program participants (e.g., constituents, readers, product purchasers). If so, who reached whom and how? • Did program participants share their enthusiasm or concerns about the program with external stakeholders or others (e.g., elected officials, newspapers, etc.). If so, who communicated what to whom and how?

Methods for Measurement

Institution to External Stakeholders

- Measure change in relationship between institution and stakeholders (identify number of board members, contributions; document baseline of the relationship).

Institution to Program Participants

- Measure institutional awareness of program participants (number of new and modified programs/venues).
- Measure change in program participants' utilization of institution (document baseline participation levels).

Program Participants to External Stakeholders

- Measure change in stakeholder relationship with program participant (better products, more programs).
- Measure change in attitude/behavior of program participant toward stakeholder (determined by nature of stakeholder).

Participants

Evaluation Rubric developed by Joel Hoffman, Paul Mohrbacher, Karen Nelson, Carolyn Sumners

Evaluation Rubric Discussion Group: Joel Hoffman, Mark Larson, Alisa Martin, Paul Mohrbacher, Karen Nelson, Paul Richard, Carolee Smith Rogers, Sarah Schultz, Sophia Siskel, Mary Ann Steiner, Carolyn Sumners, Margaret Thom

Additional Collaborators: Barbara Henry, Beth B. Schneider

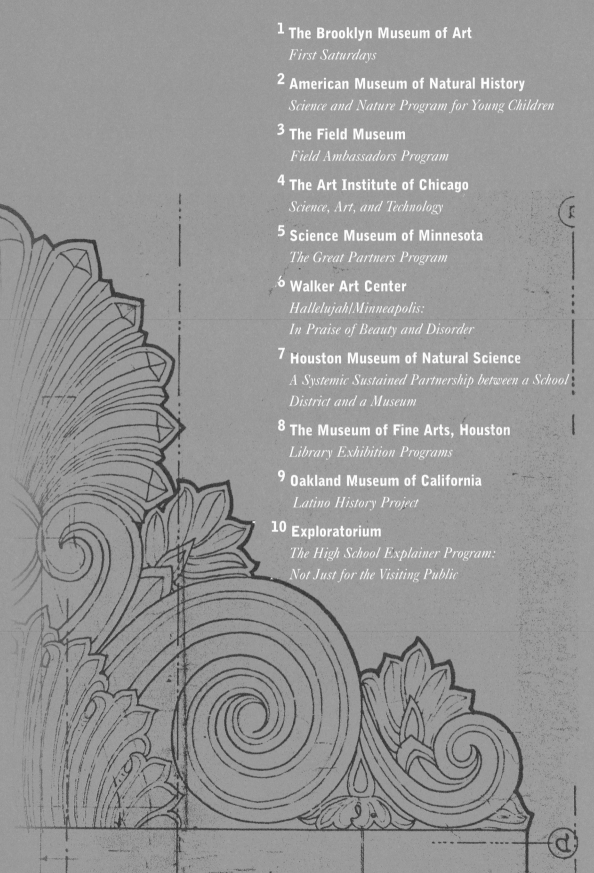

Section 5 Case Studies

The Brooklyn Museum of Art
First Saturdays

First Saturdays serve the community by creating a free, safe, fun, and educational destination for people of all ages.

"The Brooklyn Museum of Art has introduced thousands of people to the idea that museum-going can be a perfectly ordinary part of their lives."

"It's free, it's fun, and everybody's talking about it."

The whole family learns to salsa during dance lessons just before the June 2002 First Saturday dance party in the Beaux-Arts Court. *Photo by Nancy Opitz.*

Inset: Satisfied visitors leaving the family artmaking activity at the December 2002 First Saturday. *Photo by Joel Hoffman.*

The Brooklyn Museum of Art
First Saturdays

The Brooklyn Museum of Art (BMA) is the second largest art museum in New York City and one of the largest in the United States. Our permanent collection includes more than one million objects, from ancient Egyptian masterpieces to contemporary art, and represents almost every culture. The BMA is housed in a 560,000 square foot, Beaux-Arts building, and welcomes approximately 500,000 visitors each year.

Overview of Program Activities

On the first Saturday of every month except September, the museum stays open until 11 P.M. and admission after 5 P.M. is free. Galleries, cafes, and bars are open, and the museum presents educational and entertainment programs, including family artmaking activities, world music, live performances, gallery talks, films, and the extremely popular dance party. Programs showcase emerging and established Brooklyn performers whenever possible.

The Overarching Goals of First Saturdays

- To increase awareness of the BMA and its education programs in our community
- To attract new, younger, more diverse audiences
- To make people feel so comfortable and welcome that they will return to the museum again and again

Who This Program Serves

Our focus is on audiences not traditionally served by museums, including young people under 35 and people of color, particularly our nearby Afro-Caribbean community.

Objectives

- To offer a variety of educational and entertaining programs for all ages in a welcoming atmosphere
- To gain access to audiences not traditionally served by museums

Key Resources

- Spacious galleries and public areas
- Institutional support for nontraditional use of space (e.g., eating, drinking, and dancing in the Beaux-Arts Court and live performances in the galleries)
- Event committee representing all participating departments
- Sufficient staff and time to coordinate multiple adult and family programs each month

- Financial resources to produce a free event and still meet substantial budget lines for security, operations, programming, labor, public relations, and marketing

Three Key Factors Leading to Community Engagement

- Waiving admission
- Exciting, diverse programs that reflect and showcase the community
- Good public relations and marketing: "It's free, it's fun, and everybody's talking about it"

First Saturdays' Origins

In 1997, when current Director Arnold Lehman took the helm of the Brooklyn Museum of Art, annual attendance was stuck at around 300,000, less than one-third of what it had been in the 1930s, and 70 to 80 percent of those visitors were Caucasian, which did not reflect our community demographics. Museum studies showed that many Brooklynites thought we were a historical society or a children's museum. Old-timers thought we still had nature exhibitions, which had been gone for 60 years. New arrivals to the neighborhood, including the burgeoning Afro-Caribbean community, rarely crossed the street to enter the imposing McKim, Mead, and White landmark building. Clearly, we had work to do.

While most museums are in business or tourist districts, the BMA is located in the middle of residential Brooklyn. This means we're uniquely positioned to serve new audiences. It also means that it is imperative for our survival to meet community needs, particularly those of the Afro-Caribbean community moving to and living in the neighborhoods adjacent to us. "The neighborhood has changed," BMA Director Arnold Lehman told the *Guardian* (Manchester, U.K.). "This is where the museum exists, and we can't—and won't—pretend we're somewhere else."

Even before Lehman assumed his post here, the BMA made the decision to extend its hours to 9 P.M. every Saturday evening and offer music and other special free programs—though the $4 museum admission was charged. The Metropolitan Museum of Art, followed by the Museum of Modern Art, had already launched successful after-hours programs with live music on Friday nights.

This initiative commenced on May 17, 1997, in part to celebrate the museum's 100th anniversary in its landmark building and the 175th anniversary of its founding. Billed as a "Saturday Night Soirée," the event included films, music, storytelling, poetry readings, and gallery tours. Philip Morris Companies helped sponsor a marketing campaign including full-page color ads with the slogan "We're not just one of the world's great art museums. Now we're also a great night out."

The museum was disappointed in attendance during the first six months, which averaged 200 and never rose above 500, despite a second ad campaign in the fall. The press was picking up on the hip, unconventional nature of our events, including a karaoke night, which from the start was very different than the glittery, upscale after-hours affairs at the Manhattan museums.

First Saturday Is Born

To boost attendance, the BMA announced in August 1998 that it would now be open until 11 P.M. on the first Saturday of the month and admission would be free starting at 5 P.M. These new "First Saturdays" would offer music, film, gallery tours, and dance parties featuring Brooklyn bands playing different music each month. Other Saturdays, the museum would close at 6 P.M.

"Remaining open much later on First Saturdays gives the BMA the opportunity to focus its energies on providing the kind of programming requested by our public," Lehman told the press.

What better way to make friends with our neighbors than to throw a big party every month? We hoped that if they liked what they found, they would return. First Saturdays serve the Brooklyn Museum of Art's mission by revolutionizing the community's idea of a visit to a museum and by making the institution a dynamic, innovative, entertaining, and welcoming center for gathering and learning.

The BMA's first First Saturday on October 3, 1998, benefited from substantial advance play in the local media. In addition, Con Edison included a notice about the event in every Brooklyn resident's electric bill. A new colorful banner touting "Free First Saturdays" was placed on the BMA façade. Staff organized programs for the inaugural event, including an accordion band, a screening of short silent comedies with live music, storytelling in a Persian art exhibition, and a salsa and swing dance party in the Grand Lobby.

The big night arrived. Despite torrential rains, a whopping 2,000 people turned up—nearly ten times the average crowd drawn to the old weekly after-hours events. The dance party drew the biggest crowd. "Dancers ranging from infants in snugglies held between parents to young singles and older adults swung to the music of a live dance band," reported a local paper.

The next First Saturday in November dawned cool but clear. Programs included Afro-Cuban music, a book signing, gallery talks, a Fellini film, and a Caribbean dance band. By 8:15 P.M. the parking lot was full. By 9:30 P.M. attendance had surpassed 4,000, and museum security had to hold newcomers at the door. Food and drink supplies ran out. Event staff and security guards felt overwhelmed but excited. Clearly, we had a hit in the making.

Survey Results and Further Development

In all, 10,200 people attended the first three events; of those, Visitor Services surveyed 1,500 and interviewed 60. About 71 percent of those surveyed were from Brooklyn, representing nearly every part of the borough, though most came from neighborhoods closest to the museum. More than 30 percent were 18 to 35 years old, and 33 percent identified themselves as African-American, Afro-Caribbean, Hispanic, Asian or "international." About one-quarter had children under 18, and half of them had brought their children to the event. Between October and December 1998, first-time visitors at First Saturdays increased from 16 to 23 percent. In interviews, most visitors reported that they had been attracted by a specific program or by the variety of things to do. Nearly all mentioned that free admission was part of the reason they came.

By January 1999, the basic program schedule had solidified: world music from 6–9 P.M.; a film or performance in the auditorium at 7 P.M. for families and at 9 P.M. for adults; gallery talks throughout the evening; and a dance party from 9–11 P.M.

By spring 1999, event attendance had soared as high as 5,400. The press was reporting that First Saturdays had virtually eclipsed the free after-hours programs at other city museums. "The event. . . has become the biggest weekend party in Brooklyn," wrote *Brooklyn Bridge* magazine. "The talk of the borough," reported *The New York Times*. The youth-oriented weekly magazine *Time Out New York* crowed over the event's "impressively diverse crowds," coming each month "for the most jam-packed cheap dates in town." *Time Out* writer Mimi O'Connor asked: "Who knew art—or Brooklyn—could be so hip?"

Relationship with the Community

First Saturdays have shown remarkable results in building relationships between the BMA and the participants. A 2002 visitor study conducted at First Saturdays showed that 23 percent of First Saturdays' visitors were making their first visit ever to the museum in conjunction with the event—amply demonstrating the program's ability to attract new audiences, even after four years. Among those on their first visit to BMA, 79 percent felt very welcome during their visit; 69 percent indicated that they would recommend the museum to others; 65 percent expressed the intent to return to spend more time in the museum's galleries; and 74 percent considered the museum a great place to spend time with friends or family.

First Saturdays serve the community by creating a free, safe, fun, and educational destination for people of all ages. In a city where movie tickets cost $10, where tickets for concerts, theater, and sports events can soar above $100, and where babysitters often charge $20 an hour, First Saturdays provide affordable fun for the whole family. Singles and young adults also flock to First Saturdays as a safe, fun, and economical alternative to bars and nightclubs.

First Saturdays have strengthened the museum's relationships with Brooklyn performing artists and organizations. We provide a great venue, guaranteed crowd, and lots of publicity for local artists who perform at First Saturdays. Arts organizations, schools, studios, academic institutions, and bands now lobby us to showcase their artists, speakers, educators, or performers at First Saturdays. Out of these relationships, we have developed some exciting new collaborations with the Brooklyn Philharmonic Orchestra, Brooklyn International Film Festival, Brooklyn Academy of Music, Bedford Stuyvesant Restoration Dance Center, and others. Through these collaborations, the BMA is also advancing relationships between program participants and local artists and organizations.

Higher Profile

Without a doubt, First Saturdays have raised the BMA's profile in our community. The press continues to be fascinated by the First Saturdays phenomenon; the event is featured month after month as a "best pick" in the major dailies and local newspapers. It also has impacted the city's singles scene, aiding our efforts to reach young adults. In March 2001, reporters from *Time Out New York* gave First Saturdays first place on a list of the top ten creative "pickup places" in the city. While praising our dance floor and bars, *Time Out* reported that "the crowded exhibition galleries... are the museum's hottest cruising zones."

First Saturdays have received attention from the international media as well, boosting tourist attendance. In July 2001, the *Guardian* called the Brooklyn Museum of Art "a party hotspot." Reporter Joel Budd wrote, "People are shouting in the galleries, unmolested by the guards, who have relaxed their zero-tolerance policies.... Most people visit art museums because they want to have a special 'artistic' experience. The Brooklyn Museum of Art has introduced thousands of people to the idea that museum-going can be a perfectly ordinary part of their lives."

Internal Collaboration

First Saturdays have required collaboration among BMA staff on a scale never before experienced. Nearly every department in the museum has been involved, but most particularly those represented on the First Saturdays Committee: Operations, Security, Marketing and Visitor Services, Community Involvement, Education, Development/Membership, and Public Information. Committee members meet monthly to discuss the previous First Saturday and to coordinate logistics for the upcoming event; then they work with their respective departments to prepare for and implement the event.

At first, responsibilities for programming, logistics, and event implementation were divided among three departments: Adult Programs in the Education Division, Special Events, and Community Involvement. As this became unwieldy, Adult Programs assumed responsibility for booking and managing all events except for the artmaking activities, which are overseen by the Family Programs Department.

Learning from Evaluation and Experience

We use staff observations and event reports, attendance counts, and visitor research to document the program. The First Saturdays Committee and the BMA Director's Office constantly review event report findings and monthly attendance to help evaluate the program, assess problems, and find solutions.

For example, raves in the press drove attendance ever higher, and in June 1999, we set a record at 7,200. We love big crowds, but coping with these kinds of numbers presented real challenges. The lobby was too small for the burgeoning dance party, so in warmer months, we moved it to the museum parking lot. The move seemed like a good solution, but some worried that in so doing, we had separated the art from the entertainment, undermining our whole agenda to introduce people to the museum. Eventually, the museum renovated its Beaux-Arts Court and the dance party moved there; the court accommodates up to 4,000 dancers—and did so in March 2001 when we set a new record of 8,400 attendees.

Another question we faced was what to do about ticketed exhibitions. We wondered whether to make them free on First Saturdays, knowing (a) that would only increase our already big crowds when we have big blockbusters and (b) we could lose a revenue stream that we need to support these exhibitions. After trial and error, we decided that, with rare exceptions, ticketed exhibitions would remain ticketed.

Key changes in the program's early years were made as a result of evaluation:

- Galleries were kept open until the museum's closing at 11 P.M. instead of closing them at 9 P.M. This change reduced crowding in the dance party and helped support the goal of encouraging visitors to experience the art in the galleries.
- The staffing on First Saturdays was changed to include additional security staff with experience in crowd-control.
- Extra part-time staff were added to payroll each First Saturday to serve as greeters so the regular staff were not overworked during the event.
- We discontinued distributing free snacks to avoid the need for major clean-up in the galleries and to eliminate the crowd-control issues resulting from having free food.
- We discontinued the practice of hiring very well-known bands and performers to prevent overcrowding and turning away visitors. Instead, the move toward hiring local talent with their own followings has more closely linked the museum with the Brooklyn community and resulted in strong but manageable attendance.
- We introduced a monthly artmaking program based on high family attendance at the events.

Satisfied Visitors, Word-of-Mouth Promotion

During the first two years of the program, BMA staff and volunteers frequently surveyed and interviewed First Saturdays' visitors to gauge satisfaction with the program and our penetration of target audiences. In 2002, an outside firm studied First Saturdays' visitors as part of a comprehensive research effort. Research findings support maintaining the program in its present state. First Saturdays are successfully engaging an audience that is younger, often visiting in family groups, and in greater proportions of African- and Caribbean-American visitors than the traditional BMA weekday and regular weekend audience. As a free event, First Saturdays are also attracting larger numbers of visitors from lower-income households. Survey results further assure us that we are effectively engaging our Brooklyn neighbors. Travel time for over half of the visitors is under 30 minutes, with many walking or riding bicycles.

Research findings have also helped direct our marketing efforts. We learned that word-of-mouth promotion and the local distribution of postcards have been most effective in driving First Saturdays attendance. This finding has been important in the midst of budget cuts. Despite less advertising, attendance levels have remained within established ranges.

In October 2002, we launched our fourth season of First Saturdays with Target Stores as a new corporate sponsor, major support provided by Edward John Noble Foundation, and *The New York Times* as media sponsor. Despite numerous challenges in recent years, including funding cuts in the aftermath of September 11, 2001, we remain committed to welcoming our neighborhood to the museum each month at First Saturdays.

By *Joel Hoffman*, Vice Director for Education and Program Development; *Alisa Martin*, Marketing and Visitor Services Manager; and *Mona Smith*, Adult Programs Manager

American Museum of Natural History
Science and Nature Program for Young Children

Flexibility and responsiveness are key.

We use correct scientific vocabulary and introduce children to the fundamental concepts.

We included the adults as science learners as well as science educators.

Arthropod handling: Five-year-old enjoys giant tropical millipedes.
© *American Museum of Natural History/ Jane R. Kloecker.*

Inset: Arachnid observation: Louis Sorkin, Museum entomologist, works with Goddard Riverside Head Start children and their families in the after-school program.
© *American Museum of Natural History/ Jane R. Kloecker.*

American Museum of Natural History

Science and Nature Program for Young Children

Founded in 1869, the American Museum of Natural History (AMNH) is renowned for its collections and exhibitions that offer a rich record of life on earth and evidence of what we know about the universe beyond our planet. Familiar to generations for its dioramas and dinosaur bones, AMNH is also a significant research institution. Only a fraction of its 32 million artifacts and specimens are actually on display; the rest inform the work of scientists around the world, and the 200 affiliated scientists who conduct research in anthropology, biology, earth and planetary sciences, astrophysics, zoology and comparative genomics, and paleontology. The Education Department numbers more than one hundred staff, and conducts programs, creates materials, and works in collaboration with the exhibition and scientific staffs to design exhibitions and strategies for public understanding. Four million people and one-half million school children visit the American Museum of Natural History each year.

Overview of Program Activities

The Science and Nature Program engages young children, their teachers, parents, and grandparents in exploring the museum, and the science and nature of New York City, the earth, and the universe. Conducted in collaboration with community-based organizations and their Head Start programs and homeless shelters, as well as with public schools, the program provides on-site classes for children ages 3 to 9, parent and family education, and professional development for early childhood educators.

The Overarching Goals of the Science and Nature Program

The program seeks to help young children and their families and educators:

- To develop an interest in science and build a foundation for later scientific interest and inquiry
- To develop an appreciation and respect for nature

It aims to support the field, and:

- To create a model for museum-based early childhood science education, and for how to interpret the museum for younger audiences
- To mentor teachers to be confident about integrating science and nature into their classrooms, and to become independent users of the museum
- To support families learning science together
- To examine how young children learn science, and demonstrate that young children are capable of acquiring basic science skills and knowledge

Finally, the program seeks to demonstrate to the museum community that:

- Young children, from preschool age on, are a legitimate audience
  for museum exhibitions and programs
- Museums can play a critical role in providing science education to young
  children, as well as to the early childhood centers, classrooms, and
  organizations that serve them, their families, and educators

Who This Program Serves

- Children ages 3 to 9, and their significant adults, particularly those
  from underserved neighborhoods
- People of diverse ethnicities and racial backgrounds, recent
  immigrants, and a wide range of countries of origin
- Settlement houses, community organizations, homeless shelters,
  and Head Start programs
- Families who have not been museum-goers in the past

Key Resources

- Well-trained, multilingual staff with background in early childhood
  and science
- High ratio of staff to participants
- Space to set up a model early childhood classroom, rich in science
  resources, with room to display children's science-related art—and ideally,
  with light and air to house live animals and plants
- Budget that is high on personnel, science, and art supplies

Measuring for Success

- Surveys and questionnaires of participating adults
- Focus groups, interviews, and informal conversations with parents
  and teachers
- Interviews of parents and adults about their observations of the
  children's learning as well as their own learning
- Photographic record of program and activities
- External evaluation of early science learning by Edward Chittenden, Ph.D.

Three Key Factors Leading to Community Engagement

- Understanding and addressing how to make people feel comfortable
  and welcome, from food and warm greeting to educating the adults along
  with the children about the wonders of science and nature
- Focus on close and ongoing relationships with partner organizations
- Belief in young children as avid and capable science learners
  and museum explorers

The Future Meets the Past

When the idea for an early childhood science program was conceived, the American Museum of Natural History was not exactly used to the idea of little children as young scientists. Three-year-olds on expedition in Akeley Hall of African Mammals? More noise in already cacophonous halls, more strollers in already crowded elevators, and more fingerprints on diorama glass? What were we thinking!

The American Museum of Natural History has inspired generations of visitors of all ages. Ask most adults who grew up in the metropolitan region and they will inevitably recall with great affection their experiences visiting the blue whale or the giant squid or watching the stars come up in the Hayden Planetarium. For some, the Museum provided inexpensive family activities and great school field trips; for others, it was a first step in the pursuit of a career in science. Young and old found something to enjoy, and there was comfort in returning to the same scenes and halls year after year. But as science, technology, and the role of museums have evolved, it became time for AMNH to reexamine its own history, role, and responsibility to the future.

A New Era

In the past decade, the American Museum of Natural History has recast and reaffirmed its dual mission of science and education. With the building of new halls and the renovation of existing ones, the museum has made the latest scientific knowledge available to the public.

The dinosaurs were recast (literally—to reflect revised research and theories about how they actually stood and moved) and the dinosaur halls reorganized to represent physically the organization and evolution of life. The new Hall of Biodiversity captured the necessity of protecting the variation in that life. The Rose Center for Earth and Space brought the universe to light, with the Gottesman Hall of Planet Earth, Cullman Hall of the Universe, and a state-of-the-art Hayden Planetarium.

The education programs enjoyed a similar renaissance, and the institution committed to providing a continuum of programming for all ages. Starting young and instilling a lifelong appreciation for both science and the museum became an institutional priority. So did "taking the museum beyond the walls," the banner phrase of the vastly expanding education initiative. As the Science and Nature Program was beginning, planning was also under way for a new "Discovery Room," a hands-on center for children ages 5 to 12, that would serve as a gateway to the museum and introduce them to both the physical organization of the museum and its key scientific messages. Front-end research revealed a strong demand for hands-on science experiences for young children.

But for Whom?

This demand for hands-on science experiences for young children was clear among those who were already museum users, able to pay admissions costs and comfortable in this imposing institution. But there were many other people, many of whom live next door and around the corner, for whom the "gate" did not appear to swing wide open. They didn't come, and they didn't bring their children.

To bring science and the museum to these young children and their families and teachers, we began by building a relationship with a well-respected neighborhood organization, Goddard-Riverside Community Center, and its Head Start Center. A settlement house of the Jane Addams tradition, Goddard-Riverside serves low-income families, including many recent immigrants. For a substantial percentage of the families, Spanish is the first and only language. Although the Head Start Center is within walking distance, few of its staff or constituents had used the Museum. Also, like most early childhood programs, the center's classrooms were potentially rich but untapped sources of science learning. We thought that museum staff could help them capitalize on their own resources and enrich them with those of the museum.

It's About Relationships

The partnership was initiated by Myles Gordon, Vice President for Education, and Jane Kloecker, an early childhood educator and former school principal, who was hired to set up this program. Museum and Center staff worked closely together on the design and implementation. Head Start classes and educators came to the museum on a weekly basis for a full morning of classes, and museum staff went to the center nearly as often.

Curricula were planned around the new and renovated halls. The program model evolved to include expeditions in the museum, hands-on activities, science-related art projects, discussions, and guest lectures by curators, scientists, and exhibition and education staff (especially the women in these positions) to introduce the people who study science and design the halls and exhibitions.

We modeled the science for the educators, trained them, and provided materials. We included the adults as science learners as well as science educators, as we all learned together about the new halls and the science in them. We set up a bilingual mothers' group at Goddard-Riverside, "Grupo de Madres del Museo," because we saw the need for the parents to understand the science their children were learning. Many of them had had little or no education in their home countries. The Mothers Club is now made up of some original parents plus new additions each succeeding year; they treat it seriously and say they feel like scientists when they're doing microscopic studies, mounting butterflies, or dissecting owl pellets.

Guided expeditions in the Museum engage the children and adults as scientific observers and explorers. Armed with clipboards and flashlights, bands of four-year-olds, their baby brothers and sisters, Head Start teachers, parents, and grandparents fan out into the museum. In the rainforest, they shine their flashlights on each layer, looking for their assigned animals or plants, observing, drawing, and discussing their observations. In the Hall of Planet Earth, they lie down in the darkened amphitheater and watch the layers of cloud and ocean peel away from the suspended earth model, revealing the underlying structures of the earth. They feel the displayed specimens and learn about the composition and properties of rocks. They wear hard hats to the Hall of Gems and Minerals, observe the crystals, and go back to the classroom to hammer open geodes.

Our emphasis is always on the science. We use correct scientific vocabulary and introduce children to the fundamental concepts as well as to the scientists themselves. We don't "dumb down." The children can say "paleontology" before they can write it, and they know what it means.

Welcome to Our Casa

We always put effort into making our families feel they belong in the Museum and that they are wanted—an important, intangible aspect of our program. Visitors are greeted and treated with graciousness. They spread the word among their neighbors and friends, and the Museum becomes a place that they know is theirs. We give participants memberships and badges so they can move about freely and at their own pace.

It did not take long for the program to endear itself to major departments within the Museum. For the offices of Development and Communication, the program is a great place for donors to observe the Museum at work, and full of wonderful photo opportunities. But it's also becoming a favorite of the scientific staff. They appreciate that we are engaging all age groups in real science, and they are increasingly joining us in curriculum development and teaching in their areas of specialization.

Not that it has been easy. The Museum was not used to having what amounted to an early childhood center in its midst. We continually had to run interference with the security guards (would they let people in before 10 A.M.) or the maintenance staff (that's dirt for the terrarium, *not* garbage!). The biggest problem, which continued for nearly three years, was that we did not have sole rights to the classroom. By day, the room served the Science and Nature Program, but by night, it turned into a lecture hall for astronomers or geologists or conservation biologists. Every night, we had to break down the room and put away the child-size tables and chairs, not to mention the loads of science supplies, art products, drawings, and models. The millipedes went home with the Director and the tarantulas with one of the teachers; the boa constrictor spent his nights in the Vice President's office. Every morning, we put it all back again.

The Demand Is Huge

Despite these challenges, the program grew quickly, from 18 families served in the first semester of 1998 to more than 500 by the third year. New partnerships were forged with other community groups, such as Phipps Houses in the Bronx, St. Matthew's and St. Timothy's Escalera Head Start, and The Harbor for Boys and Girls, to name a few. We also began working with public schools, in our own neighborhood as well as downtown in Chinatown, where we helped them create a Discovery Garden so the children can learn about butterflies and moths, pillbugs and centipedes, and birds and non-human mammals in the middle of a heavily populated neighborhood.

These partnerships are supported by grants and donations, but we also established a set of classes that charge tuition to families that can afford to pay; both the Museum and the contributing families embrace our "Robin Hood" strategy. (The tuition and grant supported classes have now been merged.) The demand is so great that people sign up when they are pregnant. We actually received a resume from one five-year-old (more likely his parent), and given the press about what one has to do to get into a nursery school in New York City, it probably should not have been a surprise.

The Results Are Rewarding

Our real motivation is kindled by seeing results. Early evaluation data demonstrated that participants were enthusiastic about the program, loved coming, and were learning about the Museum as well as about science skills and content. In 2001, we contracted with Dr. Edward Chittenden, an expert in children's science learning. He reanalyzed the existing data, beginning with parents' perceptions of the program. More than 90 percent of the parents said that the program met their expectations, but even more revealing is information about what parents valued and why they valued it.

Parents noticed that children were making connections, showing a different kind of interest and respect, and building skills:

J. has become very aware of creatures around us: spiders, birds, and tiny fish in the water when we were in Puerto Rico. He is quite concerned about their well being.

She took my mounted butterfly from the Mother's Club to the classroom and shared it with other students.

She also explained how they grow and change. Her teacher was very impressed with her.

Her kindergarten teacher said that [my child] is a good scientist and uses her observation skills well.

My son's drawings are now much more detailed and realistic. His descriptions are more precise.

About their own learning, their comments were equally compelling:

I have learned at least as much as my son has. I was never interested in science when I was a student. I found it intimidating. Now, it somehow seems simpler and more accessible to me.

No solo los niños aprenden a cuidar a los animals, nosotros los padres también. Yo aprendí a cuidar las culebras. (Not only do the children learn how to take care of animals but the parents learn too. I learned how to take care of the snakes.)

I want to be a model for my children. I want them to see that I am a learner, so that this can motivate them as well to be learners.

The next phase of evaluation will examine the children's drawings, comments, conversations, and other indicators of what science content and skills they are learning from their exposure to this program. Chittenden is continuing with this work, and simultaneously training the teachers and parents in how to document, capture, and probe for evidence of this learning.

As we approach the future, we face a number of challenges. The specter of funding looms large. Early childhood programs are labor intensive and consequently expensive. Although we engage in substantial offsite trainings and activities, it is the use of the museum on-site that is particularly compelling and effective, and we have limited capacity to expand much beyond our current numbers. Developing materials and curricula for dissemination is a priority, yet it competes in time and resources with direct service.

What We've Learned

What are the big lessons from our experience so far? First, children can learn real science, hone their observational skills, and express in whatever medium is available and appropriate what they are seeing, hearing, and feeling. Second, a program can and should capitalize on using its halls and artifacts, collections and experts, not simply conduct hands-on science in an isolated classroom. Third, ease of access is essential: we gave the families badges and memberships so they could get in easily and move about freely; and we gave teachers memberships so they could use them on weekends and get to know the Museum better. Fourth, flexibility and responsiveness are key: the agenda of our partners takes precedence, so if they want to learn about mammals rather than geology during a given semester, we will revise our plan together; if the Museum closes a hall on a given day, we come up with an expedition to another space in the institution.

Most of all, we have learned that through welcoming people to this incredible place, we can help to instill a love of science, a love of learning, and an appreciation of the resources that are right in our families' backyard. The resources may be housed here, but in truth they belong to all of us.

By *Ellen Wahl,* Director of Youth, Family, and Community Programs; with *Jane R. Kloecker,* Director of Science and Nature Program for Young Children; and *Jean Rosenfeld,* Head Teacher, Science and Nature Program

Support for the Science and Nature Program has been provided by the Bank of America Foundation, Dickler Family Foundation, the Seinfeld Family Foundation, and the William M. and Miriam F. Meehan Foundation, Inc.

The Field Museum
Field Ambassadors Program

The Field Ambassadors Program builds links with Chicago-area schools by training educators to creatively bring Field Museum resources into their classroom teaching.

CPS school groups traditionally comprise only a small percentage of total school groups visiting the museum on field trips.

Actively developing relationships with teachers is part of the solution.

Field Museum exhibitions captivate Field Ambassador students on a school field trip. © *The Field Museum/ Mark Larson.*

Inset: Field Ambassador schools integrate The Field Museum's exhibitions into their classrooms. © *The Field Museum/ Mark Larson.*

The Field Museum

Field Ambassadors Program

The Field Museum was founded in 1893 to house and display the zoological, botanical, geological, and anthropological collections assembled for the World's Columbian Exposition. Today it is home to more than 22 million natural history specimens and cultural objects, conducts active research in almost 80 countries around the world, and presents exhibitions and education programs for a broad audience.

Who This Program Serves

The Field Ambassadors Program currently serves 184 pre-K–12 educators in 172 different schools in the City of Chicago and the surrounding region. Seventy-seven percent (141) of Field Ambassador teachers are Chicago Public School (CPS) teachers. We estimate that these teachers work directly with more than 7,050 students.

Objectives

Through the Field Ambassadors Program, we strive to improve the quality of education for more than 573,000 students enrolled in Chicago's public and private pre-K–12 schools by creating a unique professional development opportunity for their teachers. We focus the bulk of our efforts on reaching CPS teachers and schools.

Overview of Program Activities

The Field Ambassadors Program builds links with Chicago-area schools by training pre-K–12 educators to creatively bring Field Museum resources into their classroom teaching. These teachers, in turn, familiarize their colleagues with the museum as an educational resource.

Participating teachers make a two-year commitment. In their first year, they attend an orientation and a series of three Saturday forums to get to know The Field Museum and its staff, model field trip activities, engage in professional development lectures, and share ideas with one another. An end-of-year celebration recognizes the year's accomplishments and allows teachers to display the results of their collaboration and learning. To remain connected throughout the year, teachers receive a reference guide called *Field Ambassadors Handbook*, a participant directory with photographs and contact information. Teachers also receive invitations for themselves and their schools to attend museum programs, such as lectures or exhibition previews. An electronic newsletter, started in the 2002–03 year, encourages more frequent and regular communication, both between the museum and ambassadors and among ambassadors themselves.

Ambassadors who have completed their first year become members of the Field Ambassador Academy, serving as mentors for new ambassadors or advisors for education programs or exhibitions, and can elect to continue on as academy members after their two-year commitment has been met.

The Overarching Goals of the Field Ambassadors Program

- To increase The Field Museum's access to Chicago's diverse public school population
- To increase the use of museum resources by Field Ambassador schools, particularly those in the CPS system
- To create meaningful on- and off-site museum learning experiences for Chicago-area students
- To expand professional development opportunities for Chicago-area teachers
- To build relationships between The Field Museum and Chicago-area schools, so that the museum may better serve schools' needs and interests

Three Key Factors Leading to Community Engagement

- Museum staff and Field Ambassadors form personal relationships. This encourages an exchange of techniques, knowledge, and questions.
- Teachers are granted behind-the-scenes museum access, which engenders enthusiasm, understanding, and a sense of belonging to share with their students.
- Field Ambassador teachers have direct access to the city's children and can bring the Field to more than 7,000 children in hundreds of classrooms.

Key Resources

- Annual operating budget: Approximately $90,000.
- Staffing: One full-time Program Administrator has been dedicated to the program since 1999. The Program Administrator acts as the liaison between ambassadors and the museum. The Administrator plans, schedules, and manages all program events, including exhibition and behind-the-scenes tours, demonstrations, workshops, and presentations by museum professionals or outside educators. Beginning in early 2003, the Program Administrator will transition to working half time on Field Ambassadors and half time on our other teacher initiative, Museums and Public Schools (MAPS). The Field Ambassadors Program also requires part-time investment of the Manager of Student and Teacher Programs, administrative support, and participation from curatorial and exhibition staff outside of normal business hours.

- Other expenses: 22 percent of the budget is allocated to costs for meetings (parking, food, and materials). Communication-related costs, such as printing, postage, and systems technology, comprise 11 percent of the budget.
- Funding: From September 1999 through June 2003, Polk Bros. Foundation, Ryerson Tull Foundation, and Negaunee Foundation have funded the program.
- Space needs: Rooms sufficient for large gatherings, break-out rooms, and access to museum exhibition galleries and collections areas sometimes at irregular hours.
- Participant "compensation": In February 2000, in response to nationwide concerns about a shortage of qualified teachers, the Illinois State Board of Education began requiring that all Illinois teachers renew their teaching licenses every five years by engaging in high-quality professional growth activities. Field Ambassadors earn Continuing Professional Development Units (CPDUs) for the number of hours they are here for a professional development session (i.e., five CPDUs for five hours on Saturday). CPS teachers need 120 CPDUs for re-certification.
- Application process: Field Ambassadors are selected through an open application process each June. Approximately 65 percent of applicants are chosen to participate. Selection criteria include experience, leadership qualities, and school type.
- Supporting materials: We produce and distribute a *Field Ambassadors Handbook* (participant directory) and an electronic newsletter.

The Story and Measures of Success

The Field Museum's mission statement declares that we are, first and foremost, an educational institution, with the responsibility to reach and serve a visiting public that reflects the cultural, educational, and economic diversity of the Chicago metropolitan area. In 1999 a broad-based strategic planning initiative led to a set of mission-based educational goals that included:

- Developing partnerships with CPS to effectively reach the hundreds of thousands of students in this system
- Creating more effective teachers by giving them a new understanding of and relationship with the museum's resources

The Field Ambassadors Program has both of these goals at its core.

The Field Ambassadors Program was established in 1999 as a response to the real interest and need among teachers for a deeper partnership with the museum. Teachers frequently contacted us with an interest in establishing specific programs or partnerships, and we had worked with a small number of schools on isolated projects. We used this opportunity as a way to formalize how we worked with schools and to create a framework that would allow us to make a broader impact.

Field Ambassadors have grown in number from 28 to 184 over the past four years. A majority of participants teach in elementary schools. Field Ambassadors tend to be experienced teachers: 53 percent have taught for more than twenty years and only 11 percent have taught for five or fewer years. The average participant age is approximately 47, and 90 percent are female. More than half (55 percent) are Caucasian, 28 percent African American, 8 percent Latino, and 4 percent Asian American. Unfortunately, this does not mirror the demographic breakdown of all CPS teachers (where 48.2 percent are African American; 34.1 percent Caucasian; 15.5 percent Latino; 2 percent Asian/Pacific Islander; 0.3 percent Native American; and 78 percent are female); improving these ratios is one of our goals for the future.

Independent evaluators have assessed the program annually using various methods: telephone interviews with Field Ambassadors and principals at Field Ambassador schools; in-person interviews with Field Museum staff; written surveys; observation of Field Ambassador classes visiting the museum on field trips; content analysis of written communication between the museum and ambassadors, among ambassadors, and of student work; observation of Field Ambassador forums and of museum gallery and programming spaces; and Field Museum statistical data.

This evaluation has consistently demonstrated five key outcomes:

1. Use of Field Museum resources by Field Ambassador teachers has increased since the program began. At the end of the 2001–02 year:

- 65 percent indicated that their schools make more trips to the Field.
- 62 percent take their own classes more often.
- 62 percent said they use our Harris Educational Loan Center—which loans out miniature exhibition dioramas and other learning materials to teachers—more often.
- 99 percent of both teachers and principals indicated that the Field Ambassador Program improves the quality of their field trips to the museum.
- 51 percent felt that their peer teachers used Harris Loan materials more often.

2. Ninety percent of respondents said that since they became ambassadors, they enhance their lesson plans by incorporating materials from The Field Museum and 69 percent said that other teachers at their school *also* enhance their lesson plans with resources and materials from the Field. For example, one class turned their classroom into a "museum" and gave docent tours to other students and faculty; other classes designed their own exhibition guides.

3. Students' experience of these resources, whether on- or off-site, is more focused and meaningful when ambassadors use the skills they gain in the program. In

particular, ambassadors cited that their students benefited from "expanded comfort in museums"; "enhanced creativity"; "increased interest in natural history or culture"; and "strengthened connections between the classroom and real world."

4. Participation in the program has opened lines of communication among teachers in Field Ambassador schools.

5. Ambassadors are very pleased with the program and feel it to be a worthwhile and valuable professional development experience.

Tapping Into Diverse School Populations

While The Field Museum, as a world-class research institution, is an extraordinary resource for the City of Chicago, evidence suggests that it is underutilized by large sectors of Chicago's population. Unfortunately, CPS school groups traditionally comprise only a small percentage of total school groups visiting the museum on field trips. In 1998—the year before the Field Ambassadors program was launched —only 17 percent of the more than 275,000 students who visited us were from CPS.

Although museum zip code analysis indicates that close to 30 percent of our general public visitors (defined as those not attending in groups or for after-hours events) reside within the city, these visitors differ significantly from the CPS population in terms of ethnicity and income. According to museum exit research, 74 percent of our visitors are white and middle class; only 8 percent report a household income under $35,000. Eighty-five percent of the more than 437,600 CPS students live below the poverty line and only 10 percent are white.

Therefore, one of the museum's most important challenges is to increase accessibility to and interest in the museum for Chicago's most underserved youth. Since general admission is free for all Illinois schools, we believe that cost is not a factor. We believe that actively developing relationships with teachers is part of the solution. Programs such as Field Ambassadors can strengthen our relationship with a large segment of Chicago's youth by bringing museum resources and knowledge into the classroom to increase their exposure to science, world culture, and the environment.

Poised for the Future

Despite initial goals to double teacher participation every year, with an ultimate goal of having a Field Ambassador in every CPS within ten years, we have decided to pursue a more controlled growth of the program, which makes better sense both financially and logistically. Our current plan is to continue to welcome approximately 60 new ambassadors each year, 80 percent from CPS, a system that allows us to continually maintain the level of personal contact the museum has with its ambassadors—a critical factor in the success of the program.

While we cannot definitively tie increases in attendance from CPS schools to the Field Ambassadors Program, the museum has seen an increase in the percentage of CPS visits to our overall group visits since the program began—from 17 percent in 1998 to 22 percent in 2002. In 2003, our goal is 25 percent, or 77,500 of an estimated 310,000 students, from CPS.

Lessons Toward Lifelong Learning

Probably the most important lesson we have learned with the Field Ambassadors Program is that teachers really need and want guidance, and they want to serve the museum. Our evaluation shows that 99 percent of teachers participate in the program to "help The Field Museum, my school, and myself all at the same time." At the program's outset we incorrectly assumed that trained, creative teachers already knew how to incorporate museums into their lesson plans, and we simply needed to create a forum to help them do so. Since our first years when we focused on the role of the Field Ambassador and relationship building between the museum and ambassador schools, we have learned to focus on providing teachers with a forum in which to generate, share, and try out curriculum ideas with the guidance and feedback of Field Museum educators and one another. We have also begun to ask for their help by inviting ambassadors to participate in focus groups to improve the quality of upcoming exhibition designs.

We have room for improvement in keeping the ambassadors' principals involved in our programs. Evaluation of the 2001–02 year included phone interviews with principals, and we learned that they desire more direct communication about the program between themselves and the museum so that they feel more informed.

We believe that Field Ambassadors have learned, perhaps unexpectedly, that being a Field Ambassador can open lines of communication between themselves and their colleagues back in their schools. They are finding that their fellow teachers look to them as resources and are interested in communicating about museum learning, which creates possibilities for even broader dialogue. We also believe that ambassadors are surprised to learn that museums truly want to work with, and learn from, teachers—that we are not a sealed storehouse of knowledge, but a dynamic place of lifelong learning.

By *Erica Kelly*, Funding Coordinator; *Sophia Siskel*, Director of Exhibitions and Education Programs; and *Beth Crownover*, Manager of Public Programs.

The Art Institute of Chicago
Science, Art, and Technology

We designed Science, Art, and Technology to demonstrate the links between science and art for high school science teachers.

We learned the importance of including teachers and curriculum officers in the planning process from the start.

"This class makes you see how much chemistry is incorporated into art!"

Patricia Riley's chemistry student at Lincoln Park High School works in the lab on "So You Want to Buy a Painting?"
Photo courtesy of Patricia Riley.

Inset: Students from Rita Koziarski's chemistry class at Washington High School use a laptop to work on their projects.
Photo courtesy of Rita Koziarski.

The Art Institute of Chicago

Science, Art, and Technology

The Art Institute of Chicago's comprehensive collection makes it one of the leading art museums in the United States. Providing a total museum space of 376,034 square feet, the museum contains 225,000 objects ranging from ancient civilizations of Egypt, the Americas, Asia, and Europe, to paintings and sculpture from the medieval period to the present. Averaging 1.5 million visitors annually, the Art Institute is perhaps best known for its important collections of French Impressionist works and modern and contemporary art.

Overview of Program Activities

The program Science, Art, and Technology consisted of five, day-long seminars on the physics and chemistry of light and color. The program was designed by a planning committee of Art Institute and Chicago Public Schools (CPS) staff, and sessions took place at the Art Institute during the course of the 2001–02 school year.

The Overarching Goals of Science, Art, and Technology

- To address school reform by encouraging interdisciplinary teaching, critical thinking, and decision-making in the teaching of science—all of which is mandated by Illinois State Goals and specified in Chicago Academic Standards and Framework for Science (K–12)
- To reach a new audience of science teachers and students who would not otherwise visit an art museum
- To introduce these teachers to the museum's art collection as a way to enrich and inform high school science curriculum
- To inspire participating teachers to choose the museum as a meaningful field trip destination for high school students studying science

Who This Program Serves

This program was designed to reach a new audience of CPS high school science teachers. Although the course was limited to enrolled participants, the goal is to offer access to a wider audience of teachers and high school students across the country via the Science, Art, and Technology Web site developed from the contents of the course.

Objectives

- To identify common aspects of science and the humanities
- To examine how science and technology have affected or intersected art throughout history
- To demonstrate how the scientific method applies to the creation, conservation, and exhibition of works of art

- To demonstrate how the scientific method is used within a major art museum and art school in conservation, scientific testing, and artistic practice
- To provide teachers with effective teaching tools that reach students with varied learning styles and abilities
- To make teachers and students aware of the variety of careers within museums and the art world that utilize science and technology

Key Resources

- The Polk Bros. Foundation generously awarded The Art Institute of Chicago a total of $67,550 to fund this program.
- The program relied primarily on resources of the Art Institute, i.e., its collection, education staff, conservation laboratories, and publications, as well as faculty of The School of the Art Institute of Chicago.
- Other speakers included experts in the fields of science, art, and technology.

Measuring for Success

A professional evaluator utilized three research methods: pre- and post-course evaluation surveys, observations during the course by the evaluator, and three focus groups of participating teachers and their students.

Key Factors Leading to Community Engagement

We identified our immediate community to be that of the Chicago Public Schools, the nation's third largest public school system, with 440,000 culturally diverse students and 27,000 teachers.

- The involvement of the CPS Head of Science Melanie Wojtulewicz and CPS teachers and curriculum writers in the planning stages ensured that the course would be an effective classroom experience.
- Recruitment of regular CPS classroom science teachers (from non-magnet schools) ensured that course participants came from diverse school experiences. Teachers adapted the range of topics to their curriculum and produced lesson plans for in-class instruction.
- Student presentations of classroom projects at the museum in a science fair format involved the students thoroughly in the project.
- The Science, Art, and Technology Web site now allows us to reach a wider audience of teachers and students throughout the Chicago area, nationally, and internationally. Students' summative projects were documented and placed on the Web site, encouraging others to use an art museum as a source for science fair projects.

Addressing Museum Mission

To educate and inspire new and subsequent generations of artists and art lovers has always been central to the mission of The Art Institute of Chicago, which comprises a major art museum and art school granting graduate degrees in several areas of study. Educational initiatives communicate the intrinsic value and aesthetic significance of art as an expression of human thought, imagination, and creativity. Service to schools, particularly the CPS, remains an educational priority for the Art Institute.

Over the past decade, the Art Institute's division of Student and Teacher Programs has undertaken a series of year-long interdisciplinary teacher programs to support ongoing school reform efforts in the CPS. These initiatives have encouraged teaching art across the curriculum and served to bring new audiences of teachers and students to the Art Institute. To date, interdisciplinary teacher programs have explored such subjects as "Chicago: The City in Art," related to Chicago history and social studies; "Nature, Society, and Spirit," related to social studies; and "Looking to Write, Writing to See," which integrated the visual and language arts. In addition, the museum has been working for several years with Wojtulewicz on the Museum Partners Science Program. This highly successful professional development program is taught at a number of museums and intended to use each collection to secure science endorsements for middle and elementary school teachers. Building upon the accomplishments of this program, we designed Science, Art, and Technology in order to demonstrate the links between science and art for high school science teachers.

Addressing Community Needs

Teachers and students in the Chicago Public Schools, as in all large metropolitan areas, face a multitude of challenges, including limited access to exciting cultural and professional resources. This makes it particularly difficult to address school reform mandates to teach in an interdisciplinary manner. Science, Art, and Technology was designed to meet this need by showing teachers how an art museum might be used as a visual resource for teaching and learning about science. This program also allowed us to reach out to a new audience of CPS science teachers who would not ordinarily consider a visit to an art museum.

The Story

Application to the course was open to any CPS high school science teacher, but enrollment was limited, due to space constraints in the conservation laboratory. Participants were familiar with Wojtulewicz, who is highly respected for her 30-year experience as a teacher and curriculum leader. While many of the teachers had visited the Art Institute on their own, none had brought their students to the museum before the course.

As the year progressed, teachers incorporated course content into their lesson plans and oversaw the development of classroom projects by their students, who presented their projects at a culminating "Art and Science Fair" held at the Art Institute in May 2002. By the end of the course, the teachers received graduate credit and/or Continuing Professional Development Units (CPDUs).

A significant result of the program is the Science, Art, and Technology Web site connecting the museum and the School of the Art Institute to the Chicago Public Schools system. The Web site, located on the main Art Institute Web site (www.artic.edu) under "Students and Teachers," is instrumental in revealing the collection at the Art Institute and strengths of its staff to a much wider public. The course content, including lesson plans, self-guided tours, lecture summaries, books, links, and video clips, is available to all teachers who have Internet access.

In addition, the CPS student Web site will link to our online project, providing students in the CPS access to a fascinating array of materials that will enrich their studies and serve as a springboard to future science projects. We hope that the section on careers in science, art, and technology will entice an art student to learn more about science and a science whiz to learn more about art.

Planning and Implementation

In preparation for the course, we initiated a three-day planning session. Wojtulewicz selected the teachers and curriculum writers from the CPS for the planning committee. Project Director Rita McCarthy, Associate Director of Student and Teacher Programs at the Art Institute, selected a panel of planning representatives from the museum staff. Our goal for this group was to design a syllabus for the course based on the CPS program of study for science, including content area in the subjects of physics, chemistry, earth science, and biology. This group recommended that we implement a process-oriented format in line with the scientific method and inquiry-based instruction. The group decided to focus on the physics of light and color as it plays out in the making, viewing, and analysis of works of art within an art museum.

Because students and teachers learn best when they use the material and present it, planners agreed that teachers should design their own lesson plans and incorporate these into their curriculum. They would also be required to create a self-guided tour to the Art Institute for their students. Classroom projects would then be presented by students at the Art Institute. The Polk Bros. Foundation was pleased that we integrated the program into the classroom instead of structuring it exclusively as a professional development course for teachers.

Topics presented to the teachers throughout the year included Art and Astronomy; The Chemistry and Physics of Light and Color; Perception, Light, and Color; Conservation: Light in the Making and Viewing of Art; and Careers in Science, Art, and Technology. The experts on these topics included painting conservators and a conservation microscopist; School of the Art Institute professors specializing in art and technology and the perception of images; as well as a master high school physics teacher with expertise in designing and developing laboratory experiments on the physics of light and color.

The Future of Science, Art, and Technology

From Science, Art, and Technology we now have a group of CPS science teachers who are committed to the Art Institute and will continue using the museum in their teaching. The Art Institute hosted a follow-up day-long teacher workshop on the topic, which may be repeated annually and further refined.

In conjunction with the Web site, we will initiate a series of professional development programs with high school science and art teachers, utilizing the online self-guides to assist teachers in organizing a field trip for their high school science classes. These teachers will bring their students to the museum on self-conducted tours. Any new online conservation projects at the Art Institute will also be linked to this Web site for years to come (e.g., our upcoming exhibition "Seurat and the Making of *La Grande Jatte*").

The process of developing and implementing Science, Art, and Technology allowed the museum to develop lasting relationships with science administrators and teachers in the CPS. Participating science teachers developed a new understanding of what type of science goes on behind-the-scenes at the Art Institute, and they gleaned a new appreciation of works of art within the museum.

Lessons Learned

From the Art Institute's perspective:

- We learned the importance of including teachers from the start in the planning process, as well as the officers of curriculum in the schools; their input and advice was invaluable.
- The participation and endorsement of the administrator in charge of the district's science curriculum encouraged teachers to participate in the course.
- As the course progressed, teachers became active participants in developing individual curriculum for their classroom.
- Through the teachers' incorporation of content presented at The Art Institute of Chicago into the classroom curriculum, students gained exceptional insights into the science of color and light through art.

From the student participants' perspective:

"When I come [to the Art Institute], usually it's to appreciate the beauty of art. This time it was a lot more focused on content . . . and the technique of the artists. It's nice because I look and can appreciate what the art is about."—Chemistry student, Lincoln Park High School

"It was very creative to combine art and science. We noticed art such as pointillism, [in] which a million and one dots combined to make one picture."—Chemistry student, Flower Career Academy

"All the times we've had discussions before, it was always like science and art are supposed to be opposite ends of the spectrum. This class makes you see how much chemistry is incorporated into art!"—Chemistry student, Hubbard High School

By *Rita E. McCarthy*, Associate Director, Student and Teacher Programs, with *Linde Brady*, Assistant, Student and Teacher Programs, and edited by *Jane Clarke*, Associate Director of Communications

Science Museum of Minnesota
The Great Partners Program

The program has changed these organizations from consumers ... to partners in providing an affordable and enriching community resource to the families they serve.

The popularity of the ongoing program has created a strong word-of-mouth "buzz" among community groups.

The institution now has a presence on the agenda of community partners, many of which want to develop a deeper relationship.

Hands-on at the Science Museum of Minnesota.
© *Science Museum of Minnesota.*

Science Museum of Minnesota
The Great Partners Program

The Science Museum of Minnesota (SMM) is both a natural history museum with scientific research, collections, and interpretive exhibits, and a science/technology center with innovative interactive exhibitions and a hands-on learning approach. SMM is known nationally for producing traveling science exhibitions, educational IMAX films, and educational resources for students and teachers. The museum's Youth Science Center is considered a national model among museum programs for teenagers, many of whom represent traditionally underserved communities. SMM's new 400,000 square-foot museum opened in December 1999. During fiscal year 2002, more than 1.3 million individuals took part in museum programs, including roughly 150,000 on class trips.

Overview of Program Activities

Families with limited incomes can sign up to receive reduced-cost museum tickets through SMM's Great Tix Program. SMM partners with nonprofit organizations serving low-income families, called Great Partners. These organizations receive a batch of free SMM tickets once a year to be used as they wish in return for recruiting at least ten families into the Great Tix program. Offering Great Tix through Great Partners is more convenient for families who qualify for the program than signing up at the museum.

The Overarching Goal of the Great Partners Program

- To make the Science Museum more accessible to families with limited incomes

Who This Program Serves

The Great Partners Program influences nonprofits, particularly those serving community members with limited incomes, to access museum resources. The Great Tix Program targets families with an income of no more than 150 percent of the Federal Poverty Guidelines, who receive some public assistance, or who are enrolled in a state-run, sliding-scale health insurance program.

Objective

- The enthusiastic involvement of families with limited incomes as SMM visitors, members, and program participants

Key Resources

- One full-time staff person who dedicates one-third time to the project
- Clerical assistance from one part-time staff
- Involvement of two offices
- A printing and mailing budget of $1,500

Measuring for Success

The program is measured through qualitative interviews with Great Partner organizations' staff and quantitatively according to the demonstrated growth of participation, including the number of Great Partners, enrollment of families in programs, and attendance of these families to the museum.

Three Key Factors Leading to Community Engagement

- A reciprocal relationship between the Science Museum and community partners, ensuring that we each receive value from the program
- The ability of staff from community agencies to recruit families as a benefit for their clients
- Word-of-mouth endorsement among community agencies, which has been universally positive

Background

The Science Museum of Minnesota's mission is to invite learners of all ages to experience their changing world through science. For the past 20 years, the Science Museum has offered discounts to organizations that serve a limited-income audience and want to bring clients on a group visit. The organizations had a once-a-year or maybe twice-a-year relationship with the museum and saw their role only as a facilitator of group visits to the museum. The relationship was basically between the museum and the agency as a consumer of a program, Omnitheater presentation, or exhibition.

Increased Access for Families

The Great Partners Program provides easier access to the museum for families who typically could not afford to experience SMM resources. By collaborating with the staff of community organizations—including YWCAs, Boys and Girls Clubs, violence prevention programs, shelters for battered spouses, Salvation Army centers, refugee immigrant programs, family support agencies, youth programs and others—we have tapped the resources of these organizations to promote and recruit for the Great Tix discounted ticket program. In exchange, the museum helps our partners to provide community-based, leisure-time experiences for their clients. This strengthens community-museum relationships and enables low-income families to attend the museum on any day they wish.

Low-income families receive considerable discounts through the Great Tix program. For example, family members can purchase exhibition-only tickets for $1 (versus the regular prices of $8 for adults /$6 for children under 13); exhibitions and Omnitheater tickets for $3 (versus $12/$9); or exhibitions, Omnitheater, and laser-show tickets for $4 (versus $13.50/$10.50).

Families may obtain this annual card on their own by visiting the museum or mailing in a form, showing proof that they are receiving cash or medical assistance. Through Great Partners, however, our partner organizations recruit families and provide us with their names, addresses, and phone numbers. No cash is needed until the family visits the museum. The museum's marketing and sales division helped shape the program and added a half-price membership option called "Great Membership."

The program also serves clients who are adjudged by a Great Partner to be deserving even though they are not receiving any public assistance. Similarly, we have encouraged Great Partner agency staff members, particularly those in low-paying positions, to also use the discounted tickets.

Worth the Risks

The Community Relations Department, who initiated this program in consultation with the Marketing Department in April 2001, coordinated preparations for the start-up and continues to implement the program. Internally, SMM's Youth Science Center program, which offers organizations "how-to" seminars on teaching science, and SMM's diversity team played a major role in instituting the program.

The major obstacle within the museum was fear by some staff that heavily discounted tickets would erode a reliable price point for earned income. As the program grows, this continues to be a concern, but the museum chose this risk as safer than a free day, which was also discussed, because this program allows families to visit at times that are most convenient to them. Since Omnitheater shows are added when existing ones are sold out, we felt we could accommodate larger audiences, including those with discounted tickets.

Adjusting Equal Opportunities for Growth

We advertised the program through direct mail to prospective partners, including community organizations with a previous relationship with the SMM. Through personal meetings with these organizations' staffs at their headquarters, we explained the program and enrolled the agencies. The popularity of the ongoing program has created a strong word-of-mouth "buzz" among community groups. To accommodate the needs of our diverse local populations, we translated collateral materials into several languages, including Spanish, Hmong, Vietnamese, and Cambodian. We also simplified the flyer used by our partners to explain the program.

Our initial startup was rocky because we underestimated the amount of clerical support needed for the "get-the-word-out" campaign and the subsequent database entry. The museum's solution was to continue its support for families in transition by participating in a "structured work experience" for individuals returning to the work force. The program, which is grant-supported and administered by an outside agency, assists the museum with administrative and clerical support for Great Partners.

By working with community-based partners, SMM accelerated the growth of the Great Tix and Great Memberships family discount initiative, which was begun in 1996 to attract families receiving some form of public cash, food, medical, or housing subsidy. Thanks to the community partners in the Great Partners Program, enrollment and attendance have exploded, and the number of Great Partners continues to grow at the pace of three a month to a current total of 50 organizations. Income from these two programs is $20,000 annually.

In addition, enrollment for Great Tix discounts payable at the time of attendance has grown from 85 families in 1997 to 756 families in 2001 to 1,108 families in 2002. Attendance by enrollees jumped from 494 individuals in 1999 to 3,836 individuals in 2002. And, enrollment for Great Memberships at a 50 percent discount on family memberships has grown from 16 families in 1997 to 127 families in 2001 to 312 families in 2002. Attendance by enrollees increased from 794 in 2000 to 3005 in 2002.

Valuable Relationships

Based on the renewal rate, our partners are committed to the program. It has changed these organizations from consumers of an SMM group discount ticket to partners in providing an affordable and enriching community resource to the families they serve.

We learned that Great Tix participants are much more eager to sign up through a community agency with which they have an existing relationship than they are to show a benefit card that proves low-income status to a museum cashier. Clients see their agencies as providing a real service to them by recruiting for the Great Tix program on-site in their own neighborhood in a nonthreatening way.

Participant families use their Great Tix/Great Membership cards to come to the Science Museum on their own in a way they did not before. The participant card encourages frequent visits, giving the family an identity with the museum not perceived before, in addition to access to the museum.

The Great Partners Program is a museum-wide initiative, not just a discount program of the Marketing Department. The program is seen as the museum's most important tool for guaranteeing equity and access for low-income visitors.

The program has also brought value to departments within the museum, through a "ripple" effect. Our Great Partners are sought after by other youth-serving programs at the museum. We are developing "family fun nights" using the partners as the primary audience. We have developed tour-guide programs for agencies that serve audiences with English as a second language. The institution now has a presence on the agenda of community partners, many of which want to develop a deeper relationship, such as having environmental programs on the Mississippi River or after-school program support offered through the Youth Science Center.

Our perceptions of each other, museum and partner, have changed because we now know each other as mutually committed to the participants.

Consistent Growth

Our Information Services Department at the museum has been tracking participation since we established the Great Partners Program. Quantitative evaluation has demonstrated growth in enrollment and attendance of families as well as in enrollment of agencies as Great Partners. Qualitative evaluation methods at this point include anecdotal remarks by partner staff about the program's importance and "fit" for clients.

Lessons Learned Toward Increased Access

- Agencies serving low-income audiences are the best advocates for attracting low-income families to visit the museum.
- Low-income families want to come to the museum, but require a personal and trusted ally to expedite their involvement. Allies play a key function in establishing relationships with underserved audiences.
- The program is labor-intensive and requires significant staff administrative time.
- Serving a low-income audience can be a very straightforward process, without the nuances required in appealing to diverse audiences. We find it much easier to put together a program that appeals to audience on the basis of income than on the basis of ethnic/cultural differences.

From the Science Museum's perspective, the success of Great Partners introduces opportunities for variations on the program that are yet to be explored. We believe the museum is ready to build on its relationships with community partners, who we see as critical allies in reaching important audiences.

From the community's perspective, the museum is seen as committed to serving partner audiences. The community now has an "in" with the museum that will serve as an incentive to develop other programs of value to their clients.

By *Paul Mohrbacher*, Community Relations Manager

Walker Art Center
Hallelujah/Minneapolis: In Praise of Beauty and Disorder

The participants ranged in age from 10 to 87, came from diverse racial, cultural, and economic backgrounds, and had varying degrees of performance skills.

One of the most moving pieces was created in collaboration with Hmong teens trained in traditional dance.

"There is an immense pool of talent and experience among our elders who were quite fearless in taking on the project."

Hallelujah/Minneapolis: In Praise of Beauty and Disorder, Minneapolis Sculpture Garden, June 2001.
© *Walker Art Center. Photos by Dan Dennehy.*

Walker Art Center

Hallelujah/Minneapolis: In Praise of Beauty and Disorder

Walker Art Center, formally established in 1927 as the first public art gallery in the Upper Midwest, is a catalyst for the creative expression of artists and the active engagement of audiences. Focusing on the visual, performing, and media arts of our time, the Walker takes a global, multidisciplinary, and diverse approach to the creation, presentation, interpretation, collection, and preservation of art. Walker programs examine the questions that shape and inspire us as individuals, cultures, and communities.

Overview of Program Activities

Hallelujah/Minneapolis: In Praise of Beauty and Disorder was the culmination of a year-long residency by Liz Lerman Dance Exchange (LLDE) based in the Washington, D.C. area. From May 2000 through June 2001, Liz Lerman and members of her company visited the Twin Cites five times and offered local groups and individuals the opportunity to develop a performance work that reflected the participants' appreciation and celebration of everyday life. Project participants came from twelve Twin Cities community partner organizations. In addition to Dance Exchange company members, the final performance featured more than 130 artists and community members with varying performance skills. The multigenerational participants included men, women, and children from ages 10 to 87 years, who came from very diverse racial, cultural, and economic backgrounds. The Dance Exchange's workshops elicited movements and stories from participants and collaborated with them to turn them into the building blocks for the final dance performance.

The Overarching Goals of Hallelujah/Minneapolis

- To heighten audience awareness and appreciation of the Walker Art Center as a contemporary, multidisciplinary art museum and as a vital contributor to the community
- To actively engage audiences in the artist's creative process and involve them in how contemporary art encourages us to explore the issues that shape our everyday lives
- To enhance the Walker's capacity to produce multidisciplinary programs with collaborative, cross-departmental planning processes that also include community partners

Who This Program Serves

For this project, the Walker's primary audiences and partners were our neighbors who live and work in ten zip codes surrounding the Walker Art Center.

Objectives

- To provide artists an opportunity to create a performance work in collaboration with the community
- To create a community-based dance work inspired by the stories of people within the local community, and have the community participants perform the work with professional artists

Key Resources

- Walker staff from Performing Arts, Education and Community Programs Departments
- Staff resources from community partners, particularly co-presenting organizations
- Budget for the residency and presentation of the project totaling $120,530
- Rehearsal space, both at the Walker and at off-site locations
- Local dancers who served as "ambassadors" between the Walker and community partners.
- Integrated management structure between the Walker and other co-presenters
- Established communication lines between LLDE, the Walker, the community partners, and participants

Measuring for Success

We conducted qualitative evaluations that summarized the experiences of workshop participants, co-presenting organizations, and other community partners. An outside consultant conducted focus groups and evaluated the program.

Three Factors Leading to Community Engagement

- The ability of Dance Exchange company members to structure workshops to accommodate the participants' varying levels of dance experience, cultural backgrounds, and ages, and to actively engage the community in the artistic process.
- The use of participants' stories as the basis of *Hallelujah/Minneapolis: In Praise of Beauty and Disorder*, allowing the participants to take ownership of the final performance project.
- The careful design of the project to match with each community partner's organizational goals, including supporting the local dance community and multigenerational projects.

Artist Residency Involves Many Partners

In partnership with the Minnesota Dance Alliance (MDA), Intermedia Arts, and Rimon: Minnesota Council on Jewish Arts, the Walker Art Center co-presented

Liz Lerman Dance Exchange's new community-based dance-theater work, *Hallelujah/Minneapolis: In Praise of Beauty and Disorder* in June 2001 at the Minneapolis Sculpture Garden. This free performance drew nearly 1,000 audience members. Hallelujah/Minneapolis was the culmination of a year-long Liz Lerman Dance Exchange residency and was one of the largest and most complex community-based performance residencies the Walker has completed.

In addition to the four co-presenters, Hallelujah/Minneapolis involved participants from nine Twin Cities community organizations, including Arts and Religion in the Twin Cities, the Association for the Advancement of Hmong Women in Minnesota, Cathedral Basilica of St. Mary, Jeremiah Program, North High School, St. Paul Jewish Community Center, Sheridan Global Arts and Communication School, Southwest Senior Center, and Young Dance. In total, more than 130 artists and community members participated in the project. They ranged in age from 10 to 87, came from diverse racial, cultural, and economic backgrounds, and had varying degrees of performance skills. Despite the complexity and challenges of the project, the LLDE residency left a significant impact on our community members.

The co-presenters—Intermedia, MDA, Rimon, and the Walker—established a respectful and integrated partnership, which became an institution-wide role model. Led by the Walker's Performing Arts Department, these partners shared various roles throughout the year, depending on their staff and resources. Co-presenters willingly and naturally came together for this partnership as it addressed common goals held by all the organizations: a common interest in the LLDE; the opportunity to build strong ties with other organizations and communities, which would grow beyond the Hallelujah/Minneapolis experience; the desire to assemble a multigenerational group of people who would directly participate in the creative process; and a project that illuminates how contemporary art encourages us to explore the issues that shape our lives. Intermedia, MDA, and the Walker had collaborated on other projects, and the LLDE residency became another opportunity to further the partnership. Due to the complexities of the project, all the other partners who came on board had already established relationships with one or more of the co-presenters.

Hallelujah/Minneapolis, unlike many other residencies that the Walker has hosted, was deeply rooted in process. It was an organic project from the beginning, starting with an idea, and moving forward to the creation of a work with community members. The Liz Lerman Dance Exchange came to Minneapolis four times prior to their final three-week residency. During these brief visits, they met with numerous local performers, created performance work, and developed the theme for the Hallelujah project. During the last three-week period, the company finalized the performance works in conjunction with the local community and began working on-site in the Minneapolis Sculpture Garden.

Overcoming Challenges

The Hallelujah/Minneapolis: In Praise of Beauty and Disorder project grew much larger than originally anticipated. The organic nature of the residency, together with the scale and complexities of the project, presented a series of challenges for the co-presenters. It was important for LLDE to stay flexible and open to new possibilities throughout the residency so as not to exclude any potential participants. This process, however, made finalizing schedules and arranging rehearsals with participants quite difficult.

Since the performance was created for an outside venue, challenges also arose in providing technical support. As the work progressed and the technical needs became more evident, we made the necessary plans and arrangements, and shifted additional funds to cover the added expenses. As the final work was to be performed in the Minneapolis Sculpture Garden, we were totally dependent on weather. We also realized that the diversity of the participants meant that we had to plan carefully to meet a variety of special needs for rehearsal times, locations, and transportation. Until the last stage of the residency, we held workshops off-site at the locations where our community partners typically gathered (i.e., senior centers and community centers) and at times most convenient for them.

During the last two weeks, the various groups gathered together for final rehearsals at the Minneapolis Sculpture Garden. This required special arrangements to accommodate participants' various ages and needs. We needed to arrange carpools and other transportation for the young people and seniors. For seniors, we also prepared a golf cart to help them get around the Minneapolis Sculpture Garden. We needed to coordinate rehearsal times that fit the needs of working adults, seniors, students, and observant Jewish participants simultaneously. This was extremely challenging, but through persistent negotiations and compromises, we devised a rehearsal plan mostly on evenings and weekends. Rehearsal schedules shifted on a daily basis so we set up an information hotline to keep participants informed of rehearsal times, locations, announcements, and other information.

While the Walker was the key contact between the company and the local community partners, local "ambassadors" played an important role in assisting in the rehearsal process as well as disseminating information from the company and co-presenters to the participants. The ambassadors were local dancers selected and trained by the LLDE as part of the process. Two ambassadors were assigned to work with each community group participating in Hallelujah/Minneapolis. Like the LLDE, the ambassadors needed to remain flexible to work with the specific needs of their group of participants. The ambassador roles were created to be liaisons not only during the residency, but also afterwards, for the long-term impact of the project. The program allowed the local dancers selected for these roles to receive training in teaching and creating community-based dance work from LLDE, training they could incorporate into future artistic and teaching opportunities.

Feeling the Impact

The final performance was very successful despite rainy weather at our outdoor venue. The two-hour performance was condensed to ensure that the audience of nearly 1,000 would see a majority of the performance works. Originally, the performance was scheduled on Saturday, and we had Sunday as a rain date. However, when Rimon joined Hallelujah/Minneapolis, we quickly realized that we needed to move our performance date to Sunday so that Jewish participants could join the performance.

One of the most moving pieces was created in collaboration with Hmong teens trained in traditional dance. The teens and the LLDE company members worked well together because both were open and respectful of each other's process. They created a beautiful piece that utilized Hmong dancers' traditional techniques transferred into modern dance form. Members of the audience found this performance one of the most significant experiences of the production.

Following the performance, co-presenters, participants, and the LLDE expressed great satisfaction with this unique creative process. The artists' goal was to invite the participants to join them in the creation of performance work. This did happen, as did the process of starting with separate "communities" of diverse performers and turning them into one community for this final performance. The impact was deeply felt by all.

Transformations and Further Collaboration

We evaluated Hallelujah/Minneapolis in several ways. The Dance Exchange surveyed participants about their experience to identify how this program brought change into their lives. The results were profound and moving. One participant, when asked to write a postcard to future Hallelujah participants, replied: "[This experience was] more wonderful than you can imagine. You will be creating your own language of dance and movement and you will be surprised and inspired at the connections with others you will make. Watch your creativity flower in the midst of community. And it's fun."

Additional qualitative information, both informal and formal, came from surveys of co-presenters, and post-residency evaluation meetings. An outside evaluator conducted two focus groups, one held with representatives from community partners Intermedia, Rimon, and Basilica of St. Mary, and the other with twelve residency participants.

Through these evaluations, we were able to analyze the impact of the residency from multiple perspectives. David Harris, a representative from Rimon shared the following comments: "First thing to be said is that we worked very hard, had a lot of fun, and lots of people who didn't know each other had the opportunity to meet. That said, we learned that dance as an art form is still very intimidating to much of the public… We learned that time-intensive activities like Hallelujah/ Minneapolis require more advance scheduling than we were able to offer. We also learned that there is an immense pool of talent and experience among our elders who were quite fearless in taking on the project."

Numerous participants told us that through this creative residency—particularly the on-site workshops in the Minneapolis Sculpture Garden—they have a deeper relationship with the Walker, and renewed interest. One of the participants anticipated the change in her relationship by sharing the following comments: "And my relationship to this place, to the building is 'oh yeah, I've rehearsed here, I've eaten here, I've changed clothes here.' It's just a really friendly, comfortable feeling, and yet it's an impressive place too. It's not somebody's back yard. Very welcoming, making the arts welcoming in a very tangible way" (De Guzman 2002).

Many participants also expressed a sense of ownership of the project since their life stories became a source of artistic work. One of the participants shared: "I was intrigued by the process itself. Watching our stories, our comments, our experiences get translated into dance. To see from start to finish, how they put choreography together. When we performed, we were performing our own material and how we generated it from our own stories" (De Guzman 2002).

It was remarkable to see the transformation within residency participants, especially the seniors and Hmong teens, who began with very little knowledge about contemporary arts and modern dance, yet were able to articulate a personal connection to contemporary dance by the end of the process. One teenage dancer from the Association for the Advancement for Hmong Women in Minnesota, affirmed in her evaluation: "Thank you so much. I had so much fun with everyone. I'll always remember you guys and one day you'll see me dance next to you. Seeing you has opened my eyes and doors to the arts. Thank you so much for doing that. Remember me, 'cause one day you'll see me."

From the Walker's perspective, Hallelujah/Minneapolis gave us an opportunity to further and strengthen our internal and external partnerships. This project increased the partnership between the Performing Arts and Education and Community Programs Departments. The Education Department was involved from the early planning stage, and staff from these departments worked together to develop and execute this residency. In the focus group summative evaluation our partners said, "It wasn't like we were working with separate departments. We were working with the Walker on behalf of this project" (De Guzman 2002).

Externally, the Walker deepened relationships with existing partners and established some new partnerships. The relationships formed through this project have already led to several new collaborations, and we have no doubt that more will follow.

Hallelujah/Minneapolis opened new possibilities for the partners to collaborate on artistic works with each other as well. Some groups and local artists are furthering their relationship with LLDE, which continues to offer them creative opportunities beyond the *Hallelujah/Minneapolis: In Praise of Beauty and Disorder* performance. For instance, Rimon participants David Harris and Sima Rabinowitz were commissioned by the St. Paul Jewish Community Center to work with the Center's senior writers' group on the creation of a performance piece which would be built around the lives of the seniors. During October 2001 and June 2002, they developed a full-length play, *Book of Our Days*. Currently, they are exploring an opportunity to present a staged reading. Through the LLDE project, the Walker was a catalyst for the creative expression of artists and the active engagement of audiences. The legacy of the work continues in the community, even without the Walker at its center, increasing its impact exponentially.

Lessons Toward Creating a Community-Based Performance

Hallelujah/Minneapolis took many hours of planning and implementation. The complexity and scale was enormous, as was the time commitment needed to do it well. It truly challenged the capacity of our institution and the resources of our partners.

As we move on to future planning, we are all in agreement that we need to approach wisely the production of a project of this scale. This experience taught us some key elements of working with artists and the community. For a successful artist residency, it is essential that we select a project that fits the interests of our community and work with artists who truly respect the various voices of the community.

We also learned that we must let go a bit in our role as presenter and allow the process and participants to determine and shape the ultimate work, while we help to provide advice and artistic direction. That is not always easy to do, but ultimately is more rewarding and gratifying.

Work Cited

De Guzman, Marnie Burke. 2002. Walker Art Center Artists and Communities at the Crossroads summative evaluation.

By *Kiyoko Motoyama Sims*, Associate Director, Community Programs; with *Julie Voigt*, Program Administrator, Performing Arts; and *Zaraawar Mistry*, former Community Programs Coordinator

Houston Museum of Natural Science

*A Systemic Sustained Partnership between a
School District and a Museum*

**The field trip is most often the first exposure
these students have to the Houston Museum
of Natural Science.**

**The program provides all fourth-grade
students in the Houston school district with
a museum/planetarium experience.**

**Achievement gains
extended to all students
in the research study.**

Through working with specimens, students
discover how large animals really are.
© *Houston Museum of Natural Science.*

Inset: A docent explains a specimen to students
during their museum tour.
© *Houston Museum of Natural Science.*

Houston Museum of Natural Science

A Systemic Sustained Partnership between a School District and a Museum

The Houston Museum of Natural Science (HMNS) is the largest museum in the Southwest with two million annual visitors, including more than 500,000 students attending the museum in organized groups. The museum complex contains an IMAX theater, planetarium, live butterfly center, and more than 250,000 square feet of exhibitions.

Overview of Program Activities

For over thirty-five years, the Houston Museum of Natural Science has collaborated with the Houston Independent School District (HISD) on a partnership to bring additional educational resources to the district's students. The program is implemented within the school district by HISD teachers on staff at the museum and is structured according to the curricular needs of the school district.

The Overarching Goals of This Systemic Partnership

- To develop and deliver an effective museum experience addressing the academic needs of an urban school district
- To align the museum experience with the academic objectives of the school district to a level that can be considered "co-curricular"

Who This Program Serves

The program provides all fourth-grade students in HISD with a museum/planetarium experience. With the introduction of the Texas Assessment of Knowledge and Skills test for science at fifth grade, this program has refocused its academic goals to stress those areas that students must master by fifth grade.

Program Objectives

- To provide a program that remains consistent with current district curricular standards and also supplements the elementary school curriculum with experiences not available in the classroom
- To offer students the opportunity to learn science in simulated real world environments, such as the planetarium, coupled with the real world artifacts of the museum
- To increase student interest in science subjects and understanding of what a museum is (For more than 90 percent of the students in HISD, this program provides their first museum and planetarium experience.)

Key Resources

Museum exhibitions, planetarium, learning labs, and a docent program that supplies eight volunteer docents each morning. Each docent gives two tours for groups of eight to twelve students. HISD also funds 3.2 teacher salaries, divided over five museum teachers, including one full-time visiting teacher, and bus transportation for approximately 15,000 students each year.

Measuring for Success

HISD evaluates the academic performance of museum teachers each year in the same manner as it evaluates the performance of classroom teachers. Museum teachers seek feedback from visiting teachers during field trips on an informal basis throughout the school year. Formal evaluations by an independent evaluator with pre- and post-assessments are conducted whenever there is a significant change in the program.

Three Key Factors Leading to Community Engagement

Continued community engagement depends most on identifying a stable, long-term funding mechanism for staffing. Specific exhibitions, programs, and supplies can be improved through new grants over the years—provided the core staff is permanently funded. HISD's ongoing commitment to funding required personnel as part of its permanent teaching staff is the critical factor in maintaining the partnership. This commitment depends on three specific conditions:

- HISD's recognition of the value of the informal learning experience in student mastery of state and local mandated curriculum
- The museum's willingness to have programs developed and delivered by HISD staff permanently assigned to the museum
- Recognition by both partners of the value of a systemic partnership reaching an entire grade level and, in so doing, "leaving no child behind"

A Long History

The Houston Independent School District is a major urban district with more than 208,000 ethnically diverse students (56 percent Hispanic, 31 percent African American, 10 percent white, and 3 percent Asian/Pacific Islander). Over 79 percent are economically disadvantaged, and 27 percent have limited English proficiency.

The partnership between the Houston Museum of Natural Science and HISD began more than 35 years ago when the museum moved to a new five-acre tract of land in Hermann Park, in the middle of the district. At that time, HISD's need for a museum and planetarium to serve its students and the museum's new facilities led to a partnership that has continued through four museum expansions and dramatic growth and demographic change in HISD.

This systemic partnership addresses the museum's mission of education: "to preserve and advance the general knowledge of natural science and to enhance in individuals the knowledge of and delight in natural science." The museum also has an opportunity through this program to address the community's need for increased science awareness and literacy for all of its students. By making the program systemic district-wide, the museum reaches every student in HISD at the fourth-grade level.

Planning to Succeed

To guarantee the quality and appropriateness of the planetarium and museum experiences, HISD agreed to support teaching positions at the museum and a visiting teacher. These teachers develop programs and instruct HISD students during their museum field experience. Their programs must address HISD standards (now specified in a district-mandated curriculum called Project Clear), deliver the museum experiences, and be evaluated using the same protocols and criteria as other HISD teachers. As accountability standards have increased in the last decade, museum learning experiences must be increasingly tied to specific objectives and must be tested in accordance with these objectives. These teachers must meet teacher certification standards for HISD, but must also have unique skills to teach in the engaging environment of a museum or planetarium.

The continuing relationship between the museum and HISD has been maintained by a staff simultaneously accountable to HMNS and HISD. Three of the staff are full-time: two are museum teachers drawing partial salaries from HISD and HMNS. The visiting teacher is funded solely by HISD, but works out of the museum. The other two museum teachers receive pay from HISD and HMNS, but the total commitment is not full-time. Each employee is accountable for his/her time and effort to both institutions. More than anyone else, these teachers can monitor the program and make changes when needed. For content changes, these teachers work closely with HISD supervisors. Museum supervisors must approve changes in the capabilities, structure, and utilization of facilities.

Outcomes

The program has been operating in its current form since the opening of the planetarium in 1964, but student experiences have changed dramatically as the museum has expanded and the planetarium has been upgraded. Now docents have three times the number of halls for their tours and interactive hands-on carts they can use in most halls. The planetarium has evolved from a tour of the night sky to immersive moving scenes surrounding the students and operated by the planetarium teacher. The program has also adapted dynamically to changing curricular demands driven by science standards and statewide testing programs.

Enriching Our Students

The fourth-grade experience has four components. The students experience a pre-trip classroom presentation by the visiting HISD teacher from the museum. They then visit the museum for three different learning experiences: a planetarium program, a science laboratory presented by an HISD teacher at the museum, and a docent-led tour presented by volunteers. The entire museum experience lasts two-and-a-half hours with a daily maximum capacity of 150 students. Providing programs for the 15,000 fourth-grade students requires seven months. In the remaining months, the partnership offers an optional HISD seventh-grade program.

The HMNS/HISD visiting teacher reaches every fourth-grade classroom during the year. He or she normally presents interactive demonstration for a maximum of two classrooms at one time and can do three programs in a day. In HISD there are more than 675 fourth-grade classrooms to visit—requiring the entire school year. During the program, the visiting teacher prepares students for the upcoming field trip by describing what it will be like to visit the science museum and darkened planetarium chamber. This is most often the first exposure these students will have to the Houston Museum of Natural Science. The visiting teacher also introduces the topics students will experience at the museum and reinforces their prior knowledge based on concepts taught in the third grade. The presentation ends with a discussion of exciting science careers related to the museum visit.

During their 45-minute visit to the Burke Baker Planetarium, HISD's urban students have the unique opportunity to see the night sky and discover how its patterns form a tapestry on which the discoveries of modern astronomy are woven. This planetarium is the world's first to offer full-dome immersive digital video experiences. The planetarium program has been modified to address astronomy content objectives based on student grade level and encourages audience interaction.

All students also participate in a natural science laboratory designed to give them an understanding of natural science. For one hour, they become naturalists investigating real specimens from the museum's collections and analyzing adaptations of different animals to specific habitats.

In the third segment, volunteers trained by museum curators take small groups of fourth graders on 45-minute tours of the museum. During the tours, students receive personal attention from the docent tour guide, who encourages them to make observations and ask questions about exhibitions.

Preparing Teachers

The museum's HISD staff designs activities to accompany student museum experiences and provides a variety of teacher-training programs. Current curriculum activities have been bound into an activity book which the visiting teacher distributes to each fourth-grade teacher during school visits. In this way, the fourth-grade teacher has a variety of activities, from math to science, to prepare students for the field experience and to follow the museum visit.

Making a Difference

An independent formal research study of the program yielded positive results regarding the program's success. Dr. William Weber of the University of Houston conducted the study in collaboration with HISD's urban systemic initiative, funded by the National Science Foundation.

For maximum acceptability in the classroom, the test instrument was modeled on the specific multiple choice format used by the Texas Education Agency in statewide student assessment. By modeling this test design, teachers were more willing to administer the instrument as practice for the upcoming state tests. Teachers were assured that the research study would measure the effects of the museum experience and not their own instruction.

All students assigned to visit the museum during the first week of March 1999 participated in the study. Schools had been randomly assigned to this week from the entire HISD elementary school population. Therefore, results of the evaluation can be generalized to the entire HISD fourth-grade population. Table 1 describes the eight schools in the study by the percent of the student population by ethnicity and percent enrolled in the free or reduced lunch program.

Table 1: Demographics for Participating Schools
(as reported by the Texas Education Agency)

School	% white	% black	% hispanic	% in lunch program
Codwell Elementary	0.0	96.8	03.2	77.4
Concord Elementary	2.4	92.9	04.8	76.2
Douglass Elementary	0.0	96.7	03.3	98.3
Hobby Elementary	0.0	69.6	30.4	82.2
Peterson Elementary	0.0	65.6	34.4	82.8
R. Martinez Elementary	0.0	01.9	98.1	91.3
Rusk Elementary	1.6	09.8	88.5	88.5
Thompson Elementary	0.0	93.7	06.3	85.3

Students took the 45-item test one month before and within a week after their visit to the HMNS. The questionnaire first asked for demographic and anecdotal information and then had multiple-choice questions on the content from the science laboratory, the museum tour, and the planetarium. The analysis suggests that the gains made by the 438 participating students from the pretest to the posttest were both statistically significant and educationally meaningful. The results suggest that all three parts of the museum experience were effective in increasing student science achievement.

Further analysis addressed information gathered through demographic and attitudinal questions. Achievement gains in all three areas of the museum experience were *not* related to the sex of the students, their interest in science, or their prior experiences in the museum. Success on the questionnaire extended to all students in the research study.

The museum experience caused an increase in the number of students who expressed an interest in a science career (from 124 before the visit to 173 after). Students who wanted to read books about space jumped from 56 to 137.

Teachers ranked the museum experience from 1 to 5 (with 1 as unacceptable and 5 excellent). The average ranking was 4.7 for the planetarium, 4.5 for the classroom, and 4.0 for the tour. Teacher suggestions for improvement focused on the need for a longer field experience at the museum in all three areas. Only one of the 32 teachers had brought these students to the museum prior to this program.

Lessons Learned Toward Sustainability

The success and sustainability of this program over 30 years can be attributed to the integration of the HISD staff and curriculum into the museum culture. The project depends on staff accountable to both partnering institutions and aware of the needs of both institutions. The shared goal of quality science education has allowed the program to adapt as curricular and demographic changes occurred in the school district and as the museum has expanded its exhibitions and increased the learning opportunities in its planetarium and learning labs.

The program's success has led to an additional HMNS/HISD partnership for a district-wide, in-school program with a family day at second grade and a seventh-grade field trip that can include an IMAX film.

During the program's long history, HISD has evolved from a district with equal representation of black, Hispanic, and white students to a predominantly Hispanic district with the black population below 33 percent and the white population below 10 percent. In less than ten years, the HISD "at risk" population has increased from 58 percent to 79 percent. At the same time, the museum's pool of volunteer docents has dropped in size, but is still predominantly white and is now older and more likely to be retired.

The need for this program has increased dramatically as fewer of HISD's students come from families that attend the museum regularly or send children to museum classes and camps. The HISD student of today is also much less likely to have a parent or family member who is a role model for a career in science or engineering. More than before, the ultimate role of this program is to expose these urban students to real science in their world.

By *Carolyn Sumners*, Houston Museum of Natural Science Director of Youth Education and Houston Independent School District Astronomy Teacher

The Museum of Fine Arts, Houston
Library Exhibition Programs

Working with communities is not a project with a beginning and an end; it is a way to work and to think every day.

We are building relationships, not programs.

Since 1985, an exhibition from the museum has been on view in a library branch almost continuously.

Spring Branch Library Summer Art Camp with artist Wendy Miller. Children create book journals for drawing and writing. © *Museum of Fine Arts, Houston Education Department.*

Inset: A case of effigy figures, some in the shapes of animals, for the exhibition "From Playful Pups to Feathered Serpents: Animals in Ancient Mesoamerican Art," The Museum of Fine Arts, Houston, 1999–2000. © *Museum of Fine Arts, Houston Education Department.*

The Museum of Fine Arts, Houston

Library Exhibition Programs

The Museum of Fine Arts, Houston (MFAH) is a general art museum with a collection of art from around the world and from all time periods.

Overview of Program Activities

The Library Exhibition Programs bring small exhibitions of works of art from the museum's permanent collection to branches of the Houston and Harris County public libraries. Each exhibition opens at the Central Library of the Houston Public Library system, then travels to eleven other branches over a two-year period. The museum and library staff present programs at each participating branch to interpret the exhibition. As a result of this partnership between the museum and the two local library systems, we have developed other collaborative programs including art camps, after-school and homework workshops, and parent workshops.

The Overarching Goals of the Library Exhibition Programs

- To develop audiences for the visual arts and the museum
- To overcome identified barriers to museum going, such as distance, traffic, and transportation
- To develop mutually beneficial partnerships with other community organizations

Who This Program Serves

- Residents of Houston and Harris County (total population of more than 4 million people). Public library users represent the economic and ethnic diversity of the area. Library staff selects venues for each exhibition that represent a cross section of our city and county residents.

Objective

- To demystify art and museums and to emphasize that art is for everyone

Key Resources

- Good working relationships with staff in the many museum departments involved in putting together these exhibitions
- Dedicated staff at the central library administrations and at each branch
- Excellent communication among many people throughout the city and county, good logistical planning and time management skills, and enough time to make the exhibition work and to make the larger museum-library partnerships work
- A total budget of $35,000 for a two-year library exhibition program for all direct (non-staff) costs

Measuring for Success

Museum and library staff members talk with each other frequently and constantly refine joint programs. Additionally, evaluation measures include comment books for exhibition viewers and an internal library evaluation with branch managers.

Three Key Factors Leading to Community Engagement

- Strong leadership and support for this program from the museum and library directors and boards of trustees
- Flexibility and open communication between the staffs of the museum and libraries
- Great staff members throughout both organizations who are dedicated to making the program work

A Beneficial Partnership Fulfills Mutual Goals

Harris County, home of Houston, covers more than 8,778 square miles, an area larger than any other American city or the state of Rhode Island. Public transportation can be very difficult. Visitor studies conducted by The Museum of Fine Arts, Houston in the early 1990s revealed that transportation, traffic, and the great distances between many neighborhoods and the museum were barriers to museum attendance.

The Library Exhibition Program, a partnership between the MFAH and the Houston and Harris County Public Library systems, makes art accessible to library audiences throughout the region, in accordance with the museum's mission: "dedicated to excellence in collecting, exhibiting, and interpreting art for all people." Through the partnership, the library gains a wonderful program for their patrons, and the museum gains the use of exhibition spaces throughout the city and county. The partners share complementary learning and audience building goals. To achieve its goals, the museum always exhibits original works of art from its collection in order to provide the best introduction to art and the museum. It also offers programs that bring library patrons to the museum to link the library exhibitions back to the museum.

In 1974, the Education Curator, Alvia Wardlaw, developed an exhibition that traveled to six branches of the public library. Although a one-time program, it created a dialogue between the museum and the Houston Public Library. In 1985, the Education Department reinstated the Library Exhibition Program as a core project to bring the museum's collection to the the city, based on the model of a similar program at the Los Angeles County Museum of Art. Since 1985, an exhibition from the museum has been on view in a library branch almost continuously. Due to the program's success in Houston, county library staff requested that it be expanded to include the Harris County Public Library in 1998.

Library Exhibition Program Strengthens Relationships

This program requires a huge amount of teamwork and the shared belief in the importance of reaching out to new audiences by showing art in nontraditional venues. Although the Education Department drives the program, the curatorial staff develops exhibition themes and ideas. Conservators have the final say as to which objects can travel to libraries. Registrars work with the educators on various aspects of the project. The design staff creates display cases and walls to make an exhibition that can fit in libraries with very different layouts. Graphic designers create the labels, wall texts, and printed materials for the exhibition. The museum contracts a professional art moving company to move the art between branches. We have been very fortunate to have had one major funder for this program since 1993—the Wallace-Reader's Digest Fund—and additional, regular funding from Duke Energy and the Texas Commission on the Arts.

The partnership with libraries has strengthened the museum's relationships on many levels. For example, library staff members serve on a museum advisory council with representatives from community organizations and the Director of the Houston Public Library participates on the museum's Education Trustee Committee.

Planning the Exhibition

During regular meetings with our colleagues in the Houston Public Libraries (HPL) and Harris County Public Libraries (HCPL), we discuss ideas for future library exhibitions to get feedback as to what will be popular with library audiences. In the spring of each even numbered year, the Education Department sends out a request to museum curators for ideas for the next library exhibition. The curators know the kinds of objects that can go to the libraries—works that are smaller and can fit in cases or on display panels and objects that do not need highly calibrated light and climate control. Usually, the library exhibitions have consisted of three-dimensional objects. Exhibition themes have included drinking vessels in colonial America; pueblo pottery; American objects representing the life cycle from infancy to old age; containers and vessels from diverse cultures; works made by local artists in response to pieces in the museum collection; and animals in pre-Columbian art.

The Animals in Ancient Mesoamerican Art Exhibition

In 1999–2000, the exhibition "From Playful Pups to Feathered Serpents: Animals in Ancient Mesoamerican Art" traveled to a total of eleven branch libraries over a two-year period, six in the Houston Public Library system and five in the Harris Country Library system. This exhibition consisted of 21 earthenware objects, including vessels in the shapes of a monkey and a turtle, a pedestal vase with two feathered serpents, ocarinas shaped like a frog or toad, and whistles in the shapes of a curled dog, a crested bird, and a coyote head. The objects were arranged in four display cases with locking Plexiglas bonnets and decks that held the labels. A three-sided kiosk displayed the exhibition title and credit information, an introductory text for the show, and text about the museum and its community programs. A Plexiglas holder on the kiosk held flyers announcing the programs related to the exhibition at each branch. The museum produced a Spanish translation of the labels and wall texts in spiral-bound books that visitors could take through the exhibition. A comment book was mounted on a pedestal to capture visitors' responses to the exhibition.

Planning the Tour

Once the exhibition was finalized, community programs staff began working with the administrative staff for each library. For the "Animals in Ancient Mesoamerican Art" exhibition, each library system, working with their branch managers, decided which branches would receive the exhibition. They considered demographics, political districts, branch staff interest and initiative, distances between libraries and other factors in making their decisions. The two library systems, HPL and HCPL, presented the museum with the list of their venues, and together library and museum staff set up the dates for the two-year tour. Like all exhibitions, this one opened at the Central Library of the HPL, the flagship library.

Once the tour was set, MFAH, HPL, and HCPL planned an exhibition orientation for the librarians whose branches would host the show. In preparation for the orientation, museum staff assembled a loose-leaf resource binder for each branch library containing detailed exhibition information.

Exhibition-Related Programming

At the orientation, the Education Department Curator gave a slide presentation of the exhibition and MFAH staff reviewed all the logistics of moving, installing, and taking down each exhibition. Then the group discussed ideas for programming at each branch library. Librarians volunteered to compile lists of books related to the exhibition theme for story-reading programs for children or book clubs for adults, as well as to lead programs focusing on literature. After the orientation, the museum found artists, museum educators, and others to present the programs at each branch, with a special emphasis on working with the librarians to use individuals in the local community.

For the "Animals in Ancient Mesoamerican Art" exhibition, children's story-time programs included a story followed by an artmaking activity with children making animal masks, clay animal sculptures, or drawings of animals. Museum staff offered gallery talks for adult audiences. One branch requested a clay workshop for teen audiences, while another hosted a formal slide lecture on animals in Mesoamerican art.

The museum had a budget of about $1,000 for exhibition-related programming at each library venue ($5,000 or $6,000 per year). In order to give each branch flexibility, we did not allot a specific amount per branch. Rather, we asked the librarians to submit the list of programs they wanted to present, calculated the costs, and were able to meet everyone's request with the amount available because some libraries wanted only a few programs, while others wanted more. The museum paid the fees of all program presenters who were not library or museum personnel and for all art materials.

The museum printed exhibition stationery and bookmarks for the library branches to disseminate during check out. Librarians used the stationery to make flyers, printed in English and Spanish, to promote exhibition-related programs in each branch.

According to library records, 246,427 patrons viewed the "Animals in Ancient Mesoamerican Art" exhibition at eleven library branches, including 1,184 people who attended the 40 programs offered at the branches.

Library Exhibition Program Yields Further Collaborations

We know the Library Exhibition Program is successful because more library branches want to receive each exhibition than we can accommodate, comment books and informal evaluations reveal that visitors and library staff are enthusiastic about the exhibitions, and many library patrons become interested in visiting the museum. Both sets of institutions find the partnership rewarding and have raised funds to implement new programs suggested by the community libraries. This is very important because to have a truly equitable partnership, both the libraries and the museum need to be able to initiate new activities. Some of these new initiatives include:

- HCPL branch librarians bring buses of adult library patrons to museum lectures on Friday mornings. This program feeds audiences into ongoing museum activities and overcomes the transportation barrier to participation in the museum.

- HCPL asked the museum to develop summer art camps at libraries for children. Children ages 6 to 12 and their families, most from low-income communities, attend the week-long morning camps. Local artists hired by the museum lead children in daily art and literature activities, such as painting, sculpture, maskmaking and printmaking, inspired by the books that are read to them. On Wednesdays, campers and their families visit the museum for stories in the galleries, tours, and an artmaking workshop. Each camp can accommodate 25 children. In 2002 the museum presented summer camps at eight HCPL branches; 180 participated in the camp programs and an additional 160 came on the Wednesday trips to the museum. The HCPL raises money for the buses.

- In 1999, the museum began offering free admission on Saturdays and Sundays to all children ages 6 to 18 who present the HPL Power Card, or any public library card (admission to ticketed exhibitions excluded). Children who come to the museum and do not have a library card can sign up for one on the spot and receive free admission that day. We promote the library card/admission policy in all our printed materials and on our Web site.

- At the Houston Public Library, the museum is presenting parent workshops that teach adults simple artmaking activities that they can do at home with their children. These workshops, originally developed for the public schools, are offered in English and Spanish.

- In the museum, curators now approach the Education Department to ask about developing library exhibitions from their collections. For example, a grant proposal to acquire a collection of photographs from *Texas Monthly* emphasized that the collection could tour to libraries and thus reach a large and diverse audience.

Lessons Learned

Because the Library Exhibition Program is one component of a large, museum-wide commitment to presenting activities throughout the Greater Houston area, the lessons learned have come from many experiences. Here are some of those lessons from the museum's perspective:

- Taking art exhibitions to libraries in neighborhoods demonstrates the importance of neighborhood audiences. Using real works of art instead of reproductions shows a strong commitment to our audiences.
- Our commitment to community-focused programming is not dependent on grants. As long as the program meets the needs of the museum and the library, it will continue. Working with communities is not a project with a beginning and an end; it is a way to work and to think every day.
- The partnership needs to be as equal as possible. Both the museum and the libraries must commit absolutely essential aspects of the program— art and exhibition venues. Each partner must feel comfortable in asking the other to develop new programs, to modify existing programs, and to assist in related activities, etc. We are building relationships, not programs. The relationship must be able to continue even if the activities change.

By *Beth B. Schneider*, W.T. and Louise J. Moran Education Director

Oakland Museum of California
Latino History Project

The project idea was inspired by repeated concerns expressed by advisory committee members that Latino history was not being recorded or collected for future generations.

Researching community history engages teens in seeing themselves in a broader context in relation to their peers and community.

This type of museum project ignites community reunions and inspires community members to record and share their histories through social gatherings and exhibitions.

Students examine museum collections with photography curator Marcia Eymann.
Photo by Christine Lashaw.

Inset: Students problem-solve with artist Yolanda Garfias Woo to refine poster designs.
Photo by Christine Lashaw.

Oakland Museum of California

Latino History Project

The Oakland Museum of California is a major cultural institution in the San Francisco Bay Area and the only museum in the state devoted exclusively to the people, history, art, and ecology of California. Working in partnership with local schools and community advisory committees, the museum provides an extensive array of youth, family, and community education programs.

Overview of Program Activities

The Latino History Project (LHP) is a program for collecting, preserving, and exhibiting community history. It engages high school students in working with professional historians to conduct original research by gathering information through oral histories and from local community resources.

The Overarching Goals of the Latino History Project

- To address an urgent need to collect and preserve primary source materials on Latino history in the San Francisco Bay Area, including Oakland and the East Bay
- To teach high school students to research, collect, and preserve local Latino history and culture
- To inspire community members, especially young people, to see themselves as history makers—contributors to and stewards of their community's cultural heritage
- To address gaps in the museum's collections through activities that will promote further documentation, preservation, and exchange of community history
- To produce and distribute educational resources on Latino community history for broad use by schools, libraries, community organizations, and the general public

Who This Program Serves

Latino youth ages 14 to 18 participate in the program, which also encourages the broader Latino community to participate with youth in collecting the research. We also reach educators and community members interested in the region's cultural history.

Objectives

- To collect oral histories of Latino community elders, providing first-person accounts of life in Oakland and the East Bay from the early 1900s to the 1970s

- To provide historical research training for low-income Latino youth through after-school, summer, and museum internship programs
- To acquire important photographs and artifacts related to the twentieth-century history of Mexican Americans and Latinos in California for the permanent collections of the Oakland Museum of California
- To produce a Latino history Web site, an educator's handbook for collecting community history, an anthology of collected oral histories, and a series of educational posters for disseminating the project research to teachers and the broader community

Key Resources

- Staffing resources include Project Director, Coordinator/Educator, Historian, and Web Master
- Budget of $285,000, which includes costs of program staff, consultants, supplies, and production of all products (Web site, handbook, exhibitions, posters, case study, and anthology)
- Advisory committees and community elders serve as important resources
- A work space that the youth can call their own and a place where they can display their ongoing research
- Material resources include hardware and software, video camera, tape recorder, and art supplies
- Students need access to archives and collections at museums, libraries, and historical societies

Measuring for Success

Our evaluation methods are mostly qualitative. Sources include student journals with related discussions, pre- and post-tests, group discussions in research debriefing activities, questionnaires, program activities, staff observations, and team assessment sessions. The final products, including posters and exhibits, also served as valuable forms of student assessment.

Three Key Factors Leading to Community Engagement

- Partnerships or collaborations between community organizations that have influence within the local Latino community
- Involving youth as historians and "museum staff"
- Advisory committees that include elders and representatives from social service and educational organizations

Helping Youth Create a Legacy

Since the Oakland Museum of California is a regional museum dedicated to telling the stories of the people of California, the Latino History Project is central to the museum's core mission. LHP strengthens the museum's efforts by involving youth and the community in the telling of history that has never before been recorded or made available to the public. The project serves to fill in the gaps of the museum's accounts of California history, which in turn benefits all individuals wanting a comprehensive understanding of the region's cultural heritage.

Presently, few materials on the history of Latinos in the San Francisco Bay Area are available for public use. Members of the museum's Latino advisory committee expressed difficulty in finding their history represented in public educational resources such as libraries and museums. The project idea was inspired by repeated concerns expressed by committee members that Latino history was not being recorded or collected for future generations, that their history will be invisible and forgotten. LHP was initiated to address this dire need, as well as to address the frustrations of teachers unable to access Latino history resources for their students, a need made more urgent by the region's increasingly diverse student population.

Conducting LHP's original research, including oral history interviews, is crucial for documenting Latino history and culture and ensuring that a more comprehensive history of the region including the contributions of Latinos is well preserved. This research helps break down stereotypes caused by an inadequate availability of such materials. Engaging youth in this process develops their sense of stewardship for this legacy and broadens their awareness, knowledge, and skills needed to become informed citizens.

A Culture of Collaboration

LHP engages Latino youth in documenting their community's history with the help of the broader Latino community, including elders.

Collaborating community organizations included the Spanish Speaking Citizens' Foundation Youth and Family Services and the Puente Project of the University of California Office of the President. Together they provided leadership in developing and facilitating the advisory committees, identified other community members and resources to access during the project, recruited the youth, provided space for some activities, and provided ongoing counsel regarding community perspectives.

The museum's Education Department directs the LHP. The project has opened further opportunities for cooperation between education and curatorial staffs, especially with regard to merging programming with collecting initiatives.

Teaching Youth Historiography

The project was planned and implemented with support from two National Leadership Grants from the Institute of Museum and Library Services (1998–2002) and additional grants from the East Bay Community Foundation and the Evelyn and Walter Haas, Jr. Fund. During this time, two summer programs and one after-school program were conducted with three different groups of students. A Project Historian and an Educator/Coordinator were hired to work with the youth and museum education staff. The museum took the lead in coordinating the day-to-day logistics of the program.

Curatorial staff trained students in curatorial practices such as working with and caring for historical photographs, advised the Project Historian on the museum's collecting needs and guidelines, and accompanied the Historian to obtain donations.

The program itself became a laboratory for teaching youth historiography. Our hope was that through program activities students would be able to [1] conduct original historical research, [2] demonstrate increased knowledge of Latino history, and [3] demonstrate strong communication skills in presenting their historical research for public use through the creation of posters and a Web site.

Students participated in an after-school program four to five hours a week, with a stipend upon completion in June, or an eight-week summer jobs program for twenty hours a week. The after-school program took place at Hayward High School with visits to the Oakland Museum and the Hayward Area Historical Society. The summer program took place at the museum with field trips to neighborhoods, local libraries, and the City of Oakland Planning Department. The Web site instruction occurred at the Spanish Speaking Citizens' Foundation. Upon completion of the after-school or summer program, students became paid interns in the museum's Education Department.

Overcoming Challenges

Flexibility was key to the progress of this project. We regularly made changes in the scope and focus of the students' research based on students' interests, the availability of elders to interview, and the ability to locate other resources.

Keeping students on task was a challenge due to numerous factors, including the long waits involved in finding historical evidence, personnel changes, and the youth's own personal issues. The youth expressed a sense of accomplishment when they did find original historical evidence, which motivated them to persist through the difficulties of their research. The goal of sharing their historical research with a broad audience also motivated the students. Staff counseled them on how LHP mirrors the experiences of professional historians and on the details they needed to address.

Program logistics and locating resources, including the challenges of scheduling interviews with elders that accommodated student schedules, became the project staff's focus during much of the project to the detriment of other aspects of the LHP, such as a formal evaluation. Staff spent a great deal of one-on-one time with the students and were able to assess their development and growth informally. Afterwards, an evaluator assessed data collected and final products, interviewed students, and prepared a final report.

The Future of Latino History Project

As of this writing, the program is in its last phase of producing final research products for dissemination, including the following:

- A Latino history Web site, which includes a virtual exhibit of student posters and all products produced below, www.museumca.org/lhp (to be launched in spring 2003)
- A traveling exhibition featuring student posters highlighting their research
- An anthology of community stories
- Educational posters created by project team staff and consultants based on all of the research acquired throughout the programs
- A case study and an educator's handbook offering activities for engaging youth in the process of researching community history and addressing national and state school standards related to history and English/language arts

While community collaborators and staff developed initial program plans, actual implementation of program activities was shaped by responses from participants, both students and community members. Because of LHP, students reported a better understanding of community history and an increased awareness of and pride in the accomplishments of their elders. Their criticisms included the need for more training in some areas and feeling uncertain of next steps in the program. The next steps of this experimental program were based on student progress and timely availability of resources.

Lessons Learned Toward Building Community History

- A community-centered student research project requires flexibility and consistent adult involvement to address student interests as they arise through project activities. Students need to feel ownership and personal investment in their education.
- Discovering primary sources with a culminating goal of presenting their findings to the public motivates student learning and stewardship.

- Researching community history engages teens in seeing themselves in a broader context in relation to their peers and community.
- As youth historians, students develop the skills in discerning multiple perspectives and applying them to analyzing past and current events.
- Collecting community history requires strong teamwork and social interaction among all participants. Program activities need to support the development of this team as well as provide time and space for reflection.
- It is important to identify specific roles and expected contributions of each institutional collaborator, including the role of the lead institution, at every stage of a project, taking into consideration that collaborators have increased institutional demands at different times of the year.
- It is necessary to establish a variety of communication mechanisms and timely decision-making processes for involving collaborators and program participants while moving the project forward.
- Collecting community history involves sharing with community members the museum practices of collecting, documenting, and preserving materials and demystifying the practices of a museum.
- The museum is considered a neutral, comfortable place to share community history with a broader public.
- This type of museum project ignites community reunions and inspires community members to record and share their histories through social gatherings and exhibitions in public and private arenas that they themselves helped create.

In Their Own Words

"I have gained respect not only for myself but also for my ancestors. I am also very happy to know that maybe someday the work I did might be helpful to kids that, like me, didn't know much about Latino history."—Martha, age 17, LHP youth historian

"It's been beyond anything they can learn in a school day. They were able to talk to elders who actually experienced history firsthand."—Krista, LHP classroom teacher

"It can touch people. They can see something else of Latinos and not just stereotypes."—Bernardo, age 16, LHP youth historian

By *Barbara Henry*, Chief Curator of Education/LHP Director; with *Carey Fruzza*, Art Program Coordinator; and *Rachel Davidman*, Project Coordinator

Major support from the Institute of Museum and Library Services. Additional support from the East Bay Community Foundation and the Evelyn and Walter Haas, Jr. Fund.

Exploratorium

The High School Explainer Program: Not Just for the Visiting Public

As the public facilitation staff, explainers play an essential role in museum operations and the visitor experience.

High school explainers work with the public to discuss, experiment, and promote a playful atmosphere of inquiry.

It is especially important to offer youth real work opportunities and listen to participants with the intention of making change.

Exploratorium explainers in front of the Palace of Fine Arts. © *Exploratorium*.

Inset: Chris and Hector explain filters and color mixing to a young visitor. © *Exploratorium*.

Exploratorium

The High School Explainer Program: Not Just for the Visiting Public

Founded in 1969, the Exploratorium was one of world's first interactive museums. Today it houses more than 450 interactive exhibits designed by scientists, educators, and artists, and has internationally recognized programs in teacher education, youth programs, new media, exhibition design, and informal learning research.

Overview of Program Activities

Each summer, fall, and spring, the Explainer Program hires a new cohort of high school youth to work as the museum's public facilitation staff. Explainers work closely with museum staff to develop their understanding of exhibition content and facilitation. They also participate in special projects and internships to further develop their interests and experiences as teachers and facilitators for the public.

Overarching Goals of the Explainer Program

- To support the development of high school youth in teaching, science, informal learning, and other areas
- To support youth learning, confidence, and social skills through development of peer networks and work with museum staff
- To provide the museum audience with a diverse, energetic, and engaging group of young facilitators
- To increase the pool of future science educators and researchers

Who This Program Serves

The Exploratorium has served more than 3,000 students ages 14 to 20 in the Bay Area and another 200 national and international students over the past 33 years. Each year the program serves about 180 youth who are recruited to represent a broad range of backgrounds, abilities, and experiences.

Key Resources

- Staff: Program Director and two Managers, with more management during summer when youth numbers increase
- Science and exhibits development staff interested in working with youth
- Partnerships with community organizations for recruitment and collaboration
- Space: A lounge where student explainers can interact and debrief when not on the floor or in training
- Budget: $420,000 annually, two-thirds of which is floor staff salaries

Measuring for Success

Formative evaluation is conducted semi-annually and the program is adjusted as appropriate. Two summative studies have been done on the long-term impact of the program: "A Long Term Impact on Teenagers of Teaching Science to the Public," by Judy Diamond, 1987, and a longitudinal study currently conducted by Josh Gutwill and Jamie Bell, 2000–05.

Key Factors of Effective Community Youth Programs

- The program is rooted in a rich environment of educators and creative staff.
- The contribution of explainers is essential to museum operations— providing authentic avenues for youth to both contribute and learn.
- The program strives to effectively balance the needs of youth development as well as museum goals.
- The museum staff commits to and advocates for the inclusion of explainers and the program in the development of new and ongoing museum activities and programs.

Explainer Program Is Integral to the Museum's History

The High School Explainer Program began when the museum opened in 1969, at which time there were five interactive science exhibitions with one explainer. Hiring high school students as the main "education" staff of the science museum reflected the founding philosophy of the museum that science could be accessible and engaging for all visitors, despite age, gender, education, or culture. The museum aimed to provide visitors with first-hand experiences with scientific inquiry—ones that built on the visitor's own interests and sense of curiosity. The museum is designed to provide people with opportunities to generate their own questions about science and to find their own answers through discussion and inquiry. High school students provide ideal guides for this experience. They are enthusiastic about newly learned concepts, they are inclined to question and to be playful. Visitors do not perceive them as experts in the field thus reinforcing the idea that all who enter can experience and learn science. Explainers are encouraged to discover along with the visitors, rather than to provide "answers" to specific questions. High school explainers work with the public to discuss, experiment, and promote a playful atmosphere of inquiry.

The High School Explainer Program is a science youth development program, which is also key to museum operations. The program stimulates young people's interest in science and starts them on a path of noticing things around them, and looking for why things behave the way they do. The ongoing activity of noticing, contemplating, and sharing prompts reflection and discussion about their own learning.

As the public facilitation staff, explainers play an essential role in museum operations and the visitor experience. The authentic nature of their contributions to the museum is, in turn, a key aspect of the youth development program, along with participants' evolving experience as informal educators. These two sides of the coin have produced an exceptionally strong program culture, one that deeply influences and supports participating youth. The notion that visitors can benefit from novice discussions is a profound departure from traditional museum pedagogy.

Selecting and Hiring Explainers

The Exploratorium works with 180 high school-aged youth each year; these students come from a variety of diverse backgrounds, including African American, Caucasian, Hispanic, Chinese, Japanese, Cambodian, Filipino, Russian, Vietnamese, and East Indian. Approximately 70 percent of the explainers are people of color. Explainers come from all levels of socio-economic status and reflect a full range of interests and academic performance. Over 60 percent of the participants come from underserved neighborhoods.

Explainers are hired by the Program Directors. Hiring is done on the basis of developing a cohort of students who reflect a range of skills, experiences, and backgrounds. Because learning from each other is an important part of the youth development process, the balance of the group is perhaps the most critical aspect of hiring.

Hiring for a broad range of circumstances provides all of the explainers opportunities to learn from peers whom they might not otherwise encounter. It has been important for the program to constantly maintain dialogue with the museum staff in an effort to educate them about the unique character of the program that leads to different expectations as well as outcomes as compared with more traditional visitor services approaches. The program seeks people who can both contribute to the Exploratorium and help their fellow explainers to grow.

Explainers are recruited through high school teachers and counselors who refer students to the program. Some schools offer general credit to students in work experience classes. We also recruit from local community organizations that train students, look for youth employment opportunities, or are after-school centers for youth. Explainers also learn about the program by word of mouth.

The key role of the explainer is to work with visitors on the museum floor. Explainers are assigned to exhibition areas that they "roam" for set periods of time, engaging with visitors at exhibits. Explainers spend about one quarter of their time in a variety of trainings—science content, exhibition facilitation, social skills involved in approaching strangers, mediating problems or disputes, etc.—and "reflection" sessions. During these training sessions, explainers are encouraged to build from their own knowledge, experience, and instincts as budding educators.

Explainers also interact with the museum staff in a variety of ways. Informally, they have been able to provide critical feedback to the museum's exhibit design staff—discussing how visitors worked with the exhibits, reporting questions that were raised and problems that were encountered. Formally, explainers are involved in the design and development of floor demonstrations of a variety of scientific phenomena. They are also involved in the design and implementation of various youth-based and youth-oriented media projects.

During the school year, about six to seven explainers studying for their GEDs are hired to work weekdays after school. Weekend and summer cohorts range from 20 to 60 explainers. Explainers stay involved with the program anywhere from one semester to four years. The minimum commitment is four months. Every four months, a student must re-establish interest in the program by writing a letter to the program leaders. The letter is reviewed and the students are re-interviewed. Students make new goals when they commit to the program for another four months.

Reciprocal Program Provides Genuine Benefits to Museum and Youth

Explainers participate in approximately 70 hours of training during a four-month period. These sessions, conducted by staff scientists, educators, and artists, include both content and exhibition facilitation training. Initial orientation training provides explainers with an overview of the main exhibition sections of the museum, museum operation procedures, and an introduction to exhibition facilitation skills—skills that will aid them in working with the public in the museum. Ongoing training focuses on content, facilitation, and demonstration development.

Concurrent to the training, explainers work on the floor with the public. They become increasingly better equipped to talk about the exhibits and encourage visitors to explore individual exhibits as they themselves undergo their own training with the staff and talk about the concepts they have learned with the public and their peers. Their learning curve, which is repeated with each new cohort of students, reflects the dual youth development/visitor services character that we strive to maintain.

It is especially important to offer youth real work opportunities and listen to participants with the intention of making change. Giving youth real work motivates students to become more deeply engaged because in the end, they know they will be helping others—the visitors, their peers, the program leaders, and the institution.

A Unique Union: Youth and Museum Cultures

The Exploratorium High School Explainer Program is tied intimately to the museum's founding mission and has a profound and deep impact on the institutional culture of the Exploratorium. The program's longevity derives from vital discussion between participants, program leaders, and the institution. It is both a youth development program and a visitor services program. The culture of honoring youth can run contrary to widely held beliefs of what visitor services should be. For this reason, as staff have come on board over the past 32 years, we have developed the following programmatic practices to bridge understanding between museum culture and youth culture:

- Strong program leaders who can articulate the trade-offs and benefits related to such a hybrid program
- Developing internal and external staff advocates by connecting them with the explainer cohorts—through training and exhibit-centered work with staff
- Creating inroads for explainers to work with other museum projects, through internships and other means
- Developing explainer advocates through periodic reunions that bring back people to reconnect, share, and "testify" about the pivotal role the program played in their lives
- Maintaining an active leadership role in the field of education and museum operational programs for youth

Explainer Legacy Is Varied and Meaningful

The outcome of the program is as varied as each student. Every semester we have asked explainers to comment on what they have learned. Often they respond that they have learned more about people than anything else. When we then ask, "What about science?" they respond with, "yes, that too, but more about people." Our studies have shown that some students leave with an increased interest in science, while others decide they want to pursue a career in science or teaching. Many have pursued medical careers—which we speculate builds on their cultivated interest in both people and science. Some explainers have remained involved with the museum for many years, and some are now in top management positions in the museum.

The program is currently conducting a longitudinal study of a number of explainers to track how the meaning of the experience changes over time. Short-term results of this study have shown that they all remark upon what they have learned through teaching. About 62 percent comment on learning methods for teaching subject matter; 33 percent stated that they learned how to teach; and 40 percent said that they learned about tolerance. Gutwill and Bell's "Longitudinal Explainer Study" uses pre- and post-interviews to track changing values of students over a four-year period.

An earlier study conducted on the program in 1987 noted that while explainers said that they learned directly from interactions with the museum staff, half of them noted that they learned from each other. About one quarter noted that it had developed their interest in science. Dr. Judy Diamond's 1987 "A Long Term Impact on Teenagers of Teaching Science to the Public" used both quantitative and qualitative techniques. Her researchers collected background information from interview records and conducted a sample of in-person interviews and surveys. An explainer alumni comment summed up the goals of the program with this statement:

"The Exploratorium is what gave me the spark to wonder how things work and the joy when I'm finally able to figure it out. The Exploratorium had a lot to do with my decision to become an engineer and I'll always be grateful for the foundation you guys gave me. The Explainer Program to me was not just exposure to science but about exposure to new and different folks."—Explainer P.M., 1985

What the institution gains is a group of young individuals who are shaping their ideas about the world, people, culture, and science. These youth provide tremendous service to the museum and its visitors. They remind the staff of a key part of our founding mission—that science is not for the experts, that it is a process of ongoing inquiry and learning, and that it welcomes and includes all.

Works Cited

Diamond, Judy, Mark St. John, Beth Cleary, and Darlene Librero. 1987. A Long Term Impact on Teenagers of Teaching Science to the Public. *Science Education* 71 (5): 643–656. Gutwill, Josh, and Jamie Bell. 2000–05. Longitudinal Explainer Study.

By *Darlene Librero*, Director, Exploratorium High School Explainer Program; and *Bronwyn Bevan*, Director, Center for Informal Learning and Schools

Appendix

Urban Network Members

Urban Network Members

American Museum of Natural History
Central Park West at 79th Street
New York, NY 10024-5192
www.amnh.org
ph   (212) 769-5100

Myles Gordon
Vice President for Education
mylesg@amnh.org
ph   (212) 769-5172
fax (212) 769-5329

Mariet Morgan
Director for Educational
Planning and Resources
mmorgan@amnh.org
ph   (212) 496-3551
fax (212) 769-5329

Ellen Wahl
Director of Youth, Family, and
Community Programs
ewahl@amnh.org
ph   (212) 769-5142
fax (212) 769-5329

The Art Institute of Chicago
111 South Michigan Avenue
Chicago, IL 60603-6110
www.artic.edu
ph   (312) 443-3600

Robert Eskridge
The Woman's Board Endowed
Executive Director,
Museum Education
reskridge@artic.edu
ph   (312) 443-3690
fax (312) 443-0084

Jean Sousa
Associate Director of Interpretive
Exhibitions & Family Programs
jsousa@artic.edu
ph   (312) 443-3910
fax (312) 443-0084

The Brooklyn Museum of Art
200 Eastern Parkway
Brooklyn, NY 11238
www.brooklynmuseum.org
ph   (718) 638-5000

Joel Hoffman
Vice Director for Education and
Program Development
joel.hoffman@brooklynmuseum.org
ph   (718) 501-6232
fax (718) 501-6129

Alisa Martin
Marketing and Visitor Services Manager
alisa.martin@brooklynmuseum.org
ph   (718) 501-6484
fax (718) 857-6620

Exploratorium
3601 Lyon Street
San Francisco, CA 94123
www.exploratorium.org
ph   (415) 563-7337

Bronwyn Bevan
Director, Center for Informal
Learning and Schools
bronwynb@exploratorium.edu
ph   (415) 563-7337
fax (415) 561-0307

Susan Schwartzenberg
Senior Artist, Center for Media
& Communications
susans@exploratorium.edu
ph   (415) 561-0381
fax (415) 561-0370

The Field Museum
1400 South Lake Shore Drive
Chicago, IL 60605
www.fieldmuseum.org
ph   (312) 922-9410

Sophia Siskel
Director of Exhibitions and
Education Programs
ssiskel@fieldmuseum.org
ph   (312) 665-7320
fax (312) 665-7324

Beth Crownover
Manager of Public Programs
crownovr@fieldmuseum.org
ph   (312) 665-7509
fax (312) 665-7509

Patricia Williams Lessane
Diversity Project Administrator
pwilliams@fmnh.org
ph   (312) 665-7529
fax (312) 665-7529

Mary Ellen Munley
Former Director of Education

Encarnación Teurel
Former Manager of Performing Arts

Houston Museum of Natural Science
One Hermann Circle Drive
Houston, TX 77030
www.hmns.org
ph   (713) 639-4629

Lisa Rebori
    Director of Collections,
    Museum Registrar
    lrebori@hmns.org
ph   (713) 639-4670
fax   (713) 639-4767

Dr. Carolyn Sumners
    Director of Youth Education
    csumners@hmns.org
ph   (713) 639-4632
fax   (713) 639-4635

The Museum of Fine Arts, Houston
    P.O. Box 6826
    Houston, TX 77265-6826
    www.mfah.org
ph   (713) 639-7300

Beth B. Schneider
    W.T. and Louise J. Moran
    Education Director
    bschneid@mfah.org
ph   (713) 639-7321
fax   (713) 639-7707

Norma Dolcater
    Junior School Dean
    ndolcater@mfah.org
ph   (713) 639-7703
fax   (713) 639-7717

Oakland Museum of California
    1000 Oak Street
    Oakland, CA 94607
    www.museumca.org
ph   (510) 238-2200

Barbara Henry
    Chief Curator of Education
    bhenry@museumca.org
ph   (510) 238-3820
fax   (510) 238-7795

Karen Nelson
    Interpretive Specialist, Art
    karenn@museumca.org
ph   (510) 238-3005
fax   (510) 238-6925

Carolee Smith Rogers
    Interpretive Specialist, History
    csmithrogers@museumca.org
ph   (510) 238-3842
fax   (510) 238-7795

Karen Ransom Lehman
    Former Family Community Programs
    Coordinator

Science Museum of Minnesota
    120 West Kellogg Boulevard
    St. Paul, MN 55102
    www.smm.org
ph   (651) 221-9444

David Chittenden
    Vice President for Education
    davec@smm.org
ph   (651) 221-9459
fax   (651) 221-4528

Paul Mohrbacher
    Community Relations Manager
    mohrbacher@smm.org
ph   (651) 221-4745
fax   (651) 221-4777

Mary Ann Steiner
    Director, Youth Science Center
    msteiner@smm.org
ph   (651) 221-2516
fax   (651) 221-4528

Walker Art Center
    725 Vineland Place
    Minneapolis, MN 55403
    www.walkerart.org
ph   (612) 375-7622

Sarah Schultz
    Director of Education and
    Community Programs
    sarah.schultz@walkerart.org
ph   (612) 375-7621
fax   (612) 375-5802

Kiyoko Motoyama Sims
    Associate Director, Community Programs
    kiyoko.sims@walkerart.org
ph   (612) 375-7543
fax   (612) 375-5802

Amdur Spitz & Associates
    1940 West Irving Park Road, Suite 201
    Chicago, IL 60613
    www.amdurspitz.com
ph   (773) 975-1345
fax   (773) 975-0699

Jennifer Amdur Spitz
    President
    jennifer@amdurspitz.com

Margaret Thom
    Communications Manager
    margaret@amdurspitz.com

About the Editors

Jennifer Amdur Spitz is principal of Amdur Spitz & Associates, Inc. (ASA). Jennifer leads all program development and marketing communications projects for ASA. She has developed nearly a dozen new nonprofit organizations and initiatives with foundations, colleges, and museums. Jennifer has designed and executed several award-winning integrated marketing communications campaigns for ASA clients. Prior to starting ASA in 1992, Jennifer worked in government, corporate, and nonprofit communications.

Margaret Thom is a communications professional with more than fifteen years' experience. Prior to joining ASA as a Communications Manager in 2000, she worked for a foundation, an academic journal, communications firms, and nonprofit organizations.

Cover Photo Credits

Inside Front Cover (left to right)

Science Museum of Minnesota
Hands-on at the Science Museum of Minnesota.
© *Science Museum of Minnesota.*

Exploratorium
Exploratorium explainers in front of the
Palace of Fine Arts.
© *Exploratorium.*

Science Museum of Minnesota
Hands-on at the Science Museum
of Minnesota.
© *Science Museum of Minnesota.*

Walker Art Center
*Hallelujah/Minneapolis: In Praise of Beauty and
Disorder,* Minneapolis Sculpture Garden, June 2001.
Photo by Dan Dennehy. © *Walker Art Center.*

Science Museum of Minnesota
Hands-on at the Science Museum of Minnesota.
© *Science Museum of Minnesota.*

Walker Art Center
*Hallelujah/Minneapolis: In Praise of Beauty and
Disorder,* Minneapolis Sculpture Garden, June 2001.
Photo by Dan Dennehy. © *Walker Art Center.*

Houston Museum of Natural Science
During tours, docents let students touch
specimens.
© *Houston Museum of Natural Science.*

Houston Museum of Natural Science
Dinosaur skeleton on display.
© *Houston Museum of Natural Science.*

Inside Back Cover (left to right)

Exploratorium
Exploratorium explainers in front of the
Palace of Fine Arts.
© *Exploratorium.*

The Brooklyn Museum of Art
The whole family learns to salsa during dance
lessons just before the June 2002 First Saturday
dance party in the Beaux-Arts Court.
Photo by Nancy Opitz.

The Art Institute of Chicago
Students from Rita Koziarski's chemistry
class at Washington High School use a laptop to
work on their projects.
Photo courtesy of Rita Koziarski.

Walker Art Center
*Hallelujah/Minneapolis: In Praise of Beauty
and Disorder,* Minneapolis Sculpture Garden,
June 2001.
Photo by Dan Dennehy © *Walker Art Center.*

Oakland Museum of California
Historian Martin Valadez and student
review oral history transcripts to identify
useful information.
Photo by Christine Lashaw.

Houston Museum of Natural Science
Through working with specimens, students
discover how large animals really are.
© *Houston Museum of Natural Science.*

Houston Museum of Natural Science
In the science lab, students measure the
sizes of specimens.
© *Houston Museum of Natural Science.*

Oakland Museum of California
Students problem-solve with artist Yolanda
Garfias Woo to refine poster designs.
Photo by Christine Lashaw.

Walker Art Center
*Hallelujah/Minneapolis: In Praise of Beauty
and Disorder,* Minneapolis Sculpture Garden,
June 2001.
Photo by Dan Dennehy. © *Walker Art Center.*

Photo Credit
_____

end

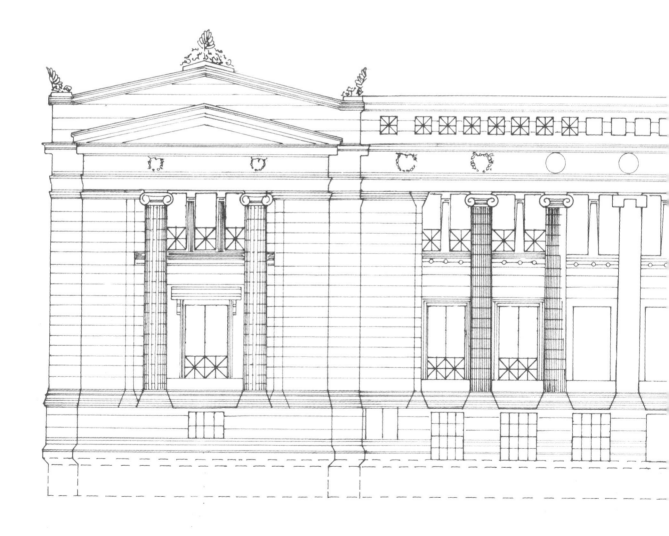

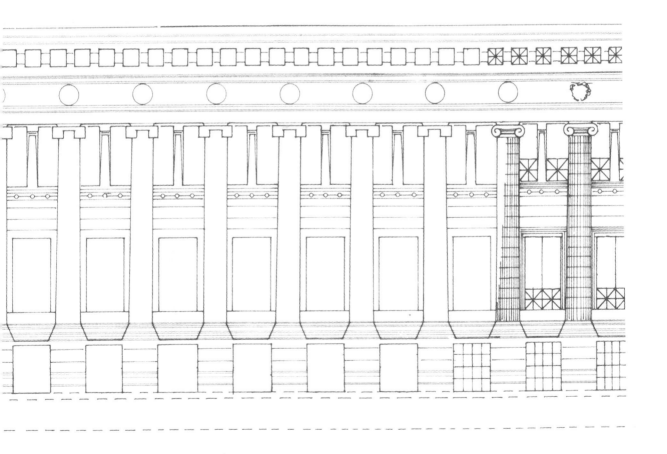